THE
BOOK OF TRADES
OR
LIBRARY
OF
USEFUL ARTS
1811

Volume I

Edited by Beryl Hurley

Published by Wiltshire Family History Society

Originally printed by
W. Flint, Old Bailey, London
for R. PHILLIPS, No. 7, Great Bridge-street.

The fourth edition, from which these trades are reproduced, was printed in 1811, in three volumes. They are now published in two volumes and the contents of Volume II are listed in the back of this volume.

Pictures are taken from *Rustic Vignettes for Artists and Craftsmen,* by W.H. Pyne, originally published in London by Rupert Ackermann & Co. in 1824, now published by Dover Publications, Inc., 180 Varick Street, New York 10014. Copyright © 1977 Dover Publications, Inc.

Wiltshire Family History Society
Registered Charity No. 290284

First published 1991
Reprinted 1992
Reprinted 1993

CONTENTS
of
PART I

Illustration on the cover is of The Gardener

THE WOOL-COMBER

The wool upon which the Wool-comber works is the hair or covering of the sheep, which when washed, and combed, and spun, and woven, makes worsted, many kinds of stuff, and other articles of great use in the concerns of life.

The wool intended for the manufacture of stuffs is brought into a state adapted for the making of worsted by the wool-comber. He first washes the wool in a trough, and, when very clean, puts one end on a fixed hook and the other on a moveable hook which he turns round with a handle, till all the moisture be drained completely out. It is then thrown lightly out into a basket. The wool-comber next throws it out very lightly into thin layers, on each of which he scatters a few drops of oil; it is then put together closely into a bin, which is placed under the bench on which he sits: at the back of the wool-bin is another and larger one for what is called the *noyles*, that is, the part of the wool that is left on the comb after the sliver is drawn out.

In each comb there are three rows of teeth parallel to one another. The best combs are manufactured at Halifax in Yorkshire: the teeth are made of highly tempered steel, and fixed into a very smooth stock, in which is inserted a handle nearly in a perpendicular position. Each workman has two of these combs: these he makes pretty hot, by putting them into a sort of jar made of clay, called a comb-pot, in which there is a fire made of the best burnt charcoal.

When the combs are hot, he puts on each a certain quantity of wool, having first disentangled it from all knots, and other obstacles that might impede the operation. He then combs the wool from off one comb on to the other alternately, till it is exceedingly smooth; when having again heated the combs, he fixes each on an iron spike placed in the wall for the purpose, and draws out the wool into a fine sliver, oftentimes five or six feet in length: what is left on the comb is called a noyle, and is fit only for the manufacture of blankets and coarse cloth.

The business of the wool-comber is different in different counties; some as the wool-combers in Hertfordshire prepare it only for worsted yarn, &c. others, as those in and near Norwich prepare it for weaving into camblets and other light stuffs.

Sometimes the worsted is required to be very white: in that case, before it is dry, after washing, it is hung up, in a close room, in which a charcoal fire is burning: on the fire some finely powdered roll-brimstone is thrown, and the room made air-tight, so as neither to admit the external air, nor suffer the vapour from the sulphur to escape.

In general, four wool-combers work at the same pot, which is made large enough to admit of eight combs. There are, of course, four distinct benches and bins of both kinds in each shop. In almost every workshop is an hour-glass, by which they measure the time: the care of this falls to the lot of a particular person. The small bottle underneath the comb is filled with oil, which is occasionally used. On the side of the wall are placed two ballads, of which in general, there are several in every wool-comber's shop.

The journeymen work by the piece, and will earn from sixteen shillings to twenty per week. Like people in many other trades, they often make holidays in the early part of the week. They come on a Monday morning, and having lighted the fire in the comb-pot, will frequently go away, and perhaps return no more till Wednesday or even Thursday. The men in this trade have a curious custom, the same with the hatters when out of work, they set out in search of a master, with a sort of certificate from their last place; this they call going on the *tramp*; and at every shop where they call, and can get no employment, they receive one penny, which is given from a common stock raised by the men of that shop. A spare bench is always provided in the shop, upon which people on *tramp* may rest themselves.

Wool-combing is preparatory to the manufacture of worsted yarn, and is the first process towards the making of flannel, serges, stuffs, baize, kerseys, &c.

The invention of wool-combing is ascribed to bishop Blaize, the patron saint of the trade, he is also of the clothiers, in honour of whom, a splendid festival is annually kept by the whole body of wool-combers in this kingdom on the third of February.

A pack of wool, which weighs 240 lbs being made into stuffs, serges, &c. it will employ 200 persons. And when made into stockings it will afford work for a week to 184 persons, viz. 10 combers, 102 spinners, winders &c. and 60 stocking-weavers, besides doublers, throwers, and a dyer.

THE SPINNER

In many country villages the art of spinning is carried on by women and children in the open air. Spinning is applied to the reducing of silk, flax, hemp, wool, hair, &c. into thread.

Spinning by hand is performed either with the distaff and spindle, or on the wheel; in the former case the person sits to her work; in the latter, she stands, or rather runs backwards and forwards. We shall describe both methods. When the distaff and spindle are used, the flax or other substance is tied or fixed on a long stick: the spinner draws out a thread which she fixes to her spindle; then with her left hand she turns the wheel, and with her right guides the thread drawn from the flax, &c. round the spindle, or rather round a spoke which goes on the spindle. When a sufficient quantity is wound on the spole, it is taken off, thrown into the basket, and replaced by an empty one.

Spinning of wool is managed by a different process. Here the wool, in those fine slivers taken from the wool-comber, is held in the hand; a thread of it is fastened to the wheel, which the spinner turns with velocity, and runs backward from it, thereby drawing out the thread to a considerable length. In either mode of spinning, when the spindle is filled, its thread is wound upon a reel, and taken off in the form of a skain or hank. The wool is delivered out to the spinner by weight, and when she returns it is again weighed. Women must be very expert who can earn at this business one shilling in a day. Children at an early age are taught the art, and will soon earn from six-pence to one and six-pence a week.

Besides the above mode of spinning wool upon the wheel, a more antient method is still practised in the county of Norfolk, with the distaff and spindle, which may be used either sitting or walking while the spinner tends on cows, poulty, &c. The sliver of wool is braided round the distaff (or *rock* as it is called by the Norfolk spinners), from the slit end which a thread is drawn and fastened to the slender spindle, which receives a whirling motion by being quickly rolled upon a piece of smooth leather called the trip-skin, fastened upon the thigh of the spinner, who with one hand gently draws a few hairs from the tail of the sliver, while the other winds up the spindle and renews its whirling motion. In this way finer yarn is made than by any other method, but more than six pence per day can seldom be earned.

Spinners are employed by the master wool-combers, whose art has been already noticed. Spinning the 'wool into skains is the next process: these are afterwards put into the hands of other women, called *winders*, whose business is, by means of a wheel and other simple apparatus, to wind two, three, or more of these skains together, so as to make a compound thread of them. This thread is wound on to spoles, or bobbins, for the convenience of having them fixed on spindles, which are turned round by mill-work in order to twist the threads, thus combined into a firm substance. When taken from the mill, the worsted is washed, dyed and dried; it is then done up in cruels, and fit for sale.

The variety and importance of those branches of our manufactures which are produced from cotton, wool, flax, spun into yarn, have occasioned many attempts to render spinning more easy, cheap, and expeditious, by mean of complicated machinery. Several of these have been very successful; particularly those for cotton by Sir Richard Arkwright; but the spinning-mill has not as yet been able to afford worsted yarn so cheap as that which is spun by hand.

The art of spinning is not confined to the human race; it is given to many animals for their preservation, as well as other purposes. Spiders, caterpillars, &c. make thread of any length that they please, by forcing the viscous liquor of which their webs are formed, through a fine perforation in the organ appointed for the work. This art is even extended to the inhabitants of the sea. The muscle possesses it in a great degree of perfection. But the method adopted by this shell-fish is very different from that made use of by caterpillars and silk-worms. The latter in their work resemble the business of the wire-drawer; the former, that of the founder who casts his metal in a mould. The canal of the organ destined for the muscle's spinning, which is called its tongue, is the mould in which the thread is cast.

."There is a species of large muscle called Pinna Marina found in the coast of Naples, Sicily, Minorca, and other islands of those seas, which by means of some wonderful contrivance of nature has the faculty of spinning, from its body, certain fine brown threads by which it fastens its shell firmly to the rocks, these threads collected form a remarkable fine kind of silk, of which stockings, gloves, and other articles in small quantities are manufactured by the people on these shores,'' Aikin's Arts of Life.

THE WATERMAN

Watermen are such as row in boats, and ply for fares on various rivers. Their business probably originated from necessity. Before bridges were erected, the intercourse which must necessarily be carried on by persons on both sides of rivers would strike out employment for a number of people who should undertake to convey persons and luggage to the opposite shore. London-bridge is of great antiquity; but Westminster-bridge has not been finished much more than half a century, and the bridge at Blackfriars was not completed till the year 1769.

A waterman requires but little to enable him to begin business, viz. a boat, a pair of oars, and a long pole with an iron point and hook at the lower end, the whole of which is not more than twenty pounds.

Sometimes two men belong to one boat; in other cases, a boat belongs to a single waterman. In the former, it is called *oars*; in the latter, it is called a *sculler*; these terms are also applicable to the oars themselves; the scull is short, and the oar is nearly double the length; from this the distinction is made of oars or sculls.

At the water side when they ply for fare the cry is *"Oars, sir." "Sculler, sir,"* according as the boat is rowed by two men or a single man. This mode of plying is chiefly confined to London.

The boat, and indeed the whole business of a waterman, on the Thames are regulated by divers acts of parliament. The names of the men who ply for fares are registered, and their boats numbered at waterman's hall; they must be twelve feet and a half long, and four feet and a half broad; and if any are found under this size they are liable to be forfeited.

No persons are allowed to ply on the river but such as have been apprentices to waterman seven years; or are at the time apprentices, and have worked with some able waterman at least two years, and are sixteen years of age.

Besides benches for the waterman, there is good accommodation for five or six persons, in the common wherry-boats.

The oars are long pieces of timber, scooped out into a thin slice at one end, and round or square at the other. That part of the oar which is out of the vessel, and which enters the water, is called the blade; the other is called the loom, the extremity of which, being small enough to be grasped by the hand, is called the handle. The place in which the oar rests is called the *row-lock*.

When there are two or more watermen in the same boat, their oars move in perfect unison; the which Shakespeare refers in his Anthony and Cleopatra:

...........*The oars were silver,*
Which to the tune of flutes kept stroke, and made
The water which they beat, to follow faster.

They have also a pole, the use of which is to push off the boat from land; a hook is fixed to one end of the pole which enables him to draw his boat to shore, or close to another boat. A post and ring are provided to moor the boats to when they are not wanted. At night a chain is passed through the ring, and the whole is rendered secure by means of a padlock.

The oval figure on the waterman's arm represents a silver badge which he has gained by his dexterity in rowing. Thomas Dogget, who was zealously attached to the house of Hanover, left by his will a sum of money to provide a *coat and silver badge* which are to be rowed for, from London-bridge to Chelsea, by six watermen, annually on the first of August, the day on which George the first ascended the throne of these realms. To the person who carries off the prize there are certain other privileges attached; one of which is, that he cannot, like other watermen, be pressed into his majesty's service. The fares of watermen are regulated by the lord mayor and aldermen, who are invested with full authority to hear and determine all complaints of acts of misbehaviour.

Most of the watermen on the Thames are employed by the fire-offices to be ready on those occasions with their water-engines, &c.

Tilt-boats, which are used for conveying passengers and luggage between London-bridge and Gravesend, are subject to strict regulations, as well as the common wherry-boats. Tilt boats must be of fifteen tons burthen: and two officers are appointed, one at Billingsgate and the other at Gravesend, to ring a bell for the tilt-boats to put off; and those which do not proceed with two sufficient men, within fifteen minutes after the ringing of the bell, are subject to a penalty of five pounds.

If any waterman between Gravesend and Windsor receive into his boat or barge a greater number of persons than the act allows, and a passenger happen to be drowned, such waterman is deemed guilty of felony, and liable to transportation.

THE BASKET-MAKER

Baskets are made of willows, which according to their manner of growth are called osiers and shallows. They thrive best in moist places; and the proprietors of such marsh land generally let what they call the willow-beds to persons who cut them at certain seasons, and prepare them for basket-makers. To form a osier bed, the land should be divided into plots six, eight, or ten feet broad, by narow ditches; and if there is a power of keeping water in these cuts at pleasure, by means of a sluice, it is highly advantageous in many seasons. Osiers planted in small spots, and along hedges will supply a farmer with hurdle stuff, as well as with a profusion of all sorts of baskets. The common osier is cut at three years, but that with yellow bark is permitted to remain a year longer.

When the osiers are cut down, those that are intended for white work, such as baskets used in washing, are to be stripped of their bark or rinds while green. This is done by means of a sharp instrument, fixed into a firm block: the osiers are passed over this, and stripped of their covering with great velocity. They are then dried, and put in bundles for sale. Before they are worked up, they must be previously soaked in water, which gives them flexibility. The basket-maker usually sits on the ground to his business, unless when the baskets are too large for him to reach their upper parts in that position.

Hampers and other coarse work are made of osiers without any previous preparation except soaking. It requires no great capital either of money or ingenuity to exercise the business of a basket-maker. Some expert workmen make a variety of articles of wicker manufacture, as work-baskets of different descriptions, table mats, fruit baskets for deserts, &c. Even in the coarser articles, a man well skilled in his trade will earn three or four shillings a day.

By some accident it once happened that a rich man and a poor pennyless basket-maker were thrown on a distant island, inhabited only by a savage race of men. The former seeing himself exposed to apparent danger, without the means of assistance or defence, and ignorant of the language of the people in whose power he was, began to cry and wring his hands in a piteous manner: but the poor man, ever accustomed to labour, made signs to the people, that he was desirous of becoming useful to them; on which account they treated him with kindness, but the other they regarded with contempt.

One of the savages found something like a fillet, with which he adorned his forehead, and seemed to think himself extremely fine. The basket-maker, taking advantage of his vanity, pulled up some reeds, and, sitting down to work, in a short time finished a very elegant wreath, which he placed upon the head of the first inhabitant he chanced to meet. This man was so pleased with his new acquisition, that he danced and capered about for joy, and ran to seek his companions, who were all struck with astonishment at this new and elegant piece of finery. It was not long before another came to the basket-maker, making signs that he also wanted to be ornamented like his companion, and with such pleasure were these chaplets received by the whole tribe, that the basket-maker was continually employed weaving them. In return for the pleasure which he conferred upon them, the grateful savages brought him every kind of food which their country afforded, built him a hut, and showed him every demonstration of gratitude and kindness. But the rich man, who possessed neither talents to please nor strength to labour, was condemned to be the basket-maker's servant, and to cut him reeds to supply the continual demand for chaplets. Such are the advantages of industry and ingenuity.

The ancient Britons were celebrated for their ingenuity in making baskets, which they exported in great numbers, they were often of very elegant workmanship, and bore a high price.

On the shores of North America is found a remarkable fish called the Basket-fish. Its body resembles that of a star-fish, and it is furnished with numerous arms to catch its prey. When caught with a hook, it clasps the bait, and encircles it with its many arms coming up in the form of a *wicker basket*, whence it has its name.

THE HAT-MAKER

Hats are made either of wool, or hair of different animals, particularly of the beaver, rabbit, and goats, but as this last is conveyed to the ports of Smyrna, Aleppo, &c. on camels, it takes the name of camels' hair. The process is nearly the same in all; it will therefore be sufficient if we describe the method made use of in the manufacture of beaver hats.

The skin of the beaver is covered with two kinds of hair, the one long, stiff and glossy; the other is short, thick set and soft, and is alone used for hats.

To tear off one of these kinds of hair, and cut the other, women are employed, who make use of two knives: a large one something like a shoe-maker's knife, for the long hair, and a smaller one nearly in the form of a pruning knife, with which they shave or scrape off the shorter hair.

When the hair is off the journeymen hat-makers mix it with the string of a bow on a table having slits in it lengthwise: and on this table they also mix the hair together, the dust and filth falling through the chinks or slits. In this manner they form sheets, or as they are called, two *capades*, or bats of an oval shape, and with the stuff that remains they supply and strengthen the parts that may be slighter than they should be. In that part of the hat which is to be next the crown, the substance is laid thicker than in the other parts.

The materials for making hats, are rabbit's fur cut off the skin, together with wool, and beaver: to which have been lately introduced mole fur, and kid hair. These are mixed in various proportions, and of different qualities according to the value of the hats intended to be made; but the beaver is now wholly used for facing the finer hats, and not for body or main stuff. Experience has shewn, that the hair or fur cannot be evenly and well felted together, unless all the fibres be first separated, or put into the same state with regard to each other. This is the object of the first process of hat-making, and is called *bowing*. The material is laid upon a platform of wood, or of wire, about four feet square called a *hurdle*, which is fixed against the wall of the work-shop, and is enlightened by a small window, and separated by two side partitions from other hurdles, which occupy the rest of the space along the wall. The hurdle, if of wood, is made of deal boards, not quite three inches wide, disposed parallel to the wall, and at the distance of one-fortieth of an inch from each other, for the purpose of suffering the dust and other impurities of the stuff, to pass through a purpose still more effectually answered by a hurdle of wire. The workman is provided with a bow, bow-pin, a basket, and several cloths. The bow is a pole of yellow deal or ash, about seven feet long, to which are fixed two bridges, somewhat like that which receives the hair in the bow of the violin. Over these is stretched a cat-gut about one-twelfth of an inch in thickness. The bow-pin is a stick with a knob, and is used for plucking the bow-string. The basket is a square piece of ozier-work, consisting of open straight bars with no crossing or interweaving; its length across the bars two feet, and its breadth eighteen inches. The sides into which the bars are fixed are slightly bent into a circular curve, so that the basket may be set upright on one of these edges, near the right-hand end of the hurdle, where it usually stands. The cloths are linen. Besides these implements, the workman is also provided with brown paper.

The *bowing* commences by shoveling the material towards the right-hand partition with the basket, upon which the workman, holding the bow horizontally in his left hand, and the bow-pin in his right, lightly places the bow-string, and gives it a pluck with the pin. The string, in its return, strikes

11

upon the fur, and causes it to spring up in the hair, and fly partly across the hurdle in a light open form. By repeated strokes, the whole is thus subjected to the bow; and this beating is repeated till all the original clots or filaments are perfectly opened and dilated, and, having thus fallen together in all possible directions, form a thin mass or substance for the felt. The quantity thus treated at once is called a *batt*, and never exceeds half the quantity required to make one hat.

When the batt is sufficiently bowed, it is ready for *hardening*; which term denotes the first commencement of felting. The prepared material, being evenly disposed on the hurdle, is first pressed down by the convex side of the basket, then covered with a cloth and pressed backwards and forwards, successively in its various parts, by the hand of the workman. This pressure brings the hairs closer to each other and multiplies their points of contract: whilst their agitation gives to each hair a progessive motion towards the root by means of this motion the hairs are twisted together, and the *lamellae* of each hair, by fixing themselves to those of other hairs, which happen to be directed the contrary way, keep the whole in compact state.

When the felt has thus acquired the necessary firmness and consistence intended to be given to it by the above mentioned agitation and pressure, the cloth is taken off, and a sheet of paper with its corner doubled in, so as to give it a triangular outline, is laid upon the batt, which last is folded over the paper as it lies, and its edges, meeting one over the other, form a conical cap. The joining is soon made good by pressure with the hands on the cloth. Another batt, ready hardened, is in the next place laid on the hurdle, and the cap here mentioned placed upon it, with the joining downwards. This last bat, being also folded up, will consequently have its place of junction diametrically opposite to that of the inner felt, which it must therefore greatly tend to strengthen. The principal part of the intended hat is thus put together, and now requires to be worked with the hands a considerable time upon the hurdle, the cloth being also occasionally sprinkled with clear water. During the whole of this operation, which is called *basoning*, the felt becomes firmer and firmer, and contracts in its dimensions. It may easily be understood, that the chief use of the paper is to prevent the sides from felting together. A superior method is said to be, that after the bowing, and previous to the basoning a hardening skin of leather, alumed or half tanned, should be used instead of the cloth, and pressed upon the batt, to bring it by an easier gradation to a compact appearance. This operation of basoning, derives its name from the process or mode of working being the same as that practised upon a wool hat after bowing; the last being done upon a piece of cast metal, three feet across of a circular shape, called a *bason*; the joining of each batt is made good here by the motion of the hand, that is, by rubbing the edges of each batt folded over the other to excite the progressive action of the filaments in felting, and to join the two together.

The basoning is followed by a still more effectual continuation of the felting, called *working*. This is done at an apparatus called *a battery*, consisting of a kettle (containing water slightly acidulated with sulphuric acid, to which, for beaver hats, a quantity of wine-lees or the grounds of beer is added, or else plain water for rinsing out), and eight planks of wood joined together in the form of a frustrum of a cone, and meeting in the kettle at the middle. The outer or upper edge of each plank is about two feet broad, and rises a little more than two feet and half above the ground; and the slope towards the kettle is considerably rapid, so that the whole battery is little more than six feet in diameter. The quantity of sulphuric acid added to the liquor is not sufficient to give a sour taste, but only renders it rough to the tongue. In this liquor, heated rather higher than unpractised hands could bear, the felt is dipped from time to time, and worked on the planks; before which it is plunged gently into the boiling kettle till fully saturated with the liquor which is called *soaking*. The imperfections of the felt present themselves in the course of this part of the work to the eye of the workman; who picks out knots and other hard substances with a bodkin, and adds more fur upon all such parts as require strengthening. This added fur is patted down with a wet brush, and soon incorporates with the rest. Many hatters to hurry this work, use a quantity of vitriol, (sulphuric acid) and then, to make the nap rise and flow, they kill or neutralize the vitriol, and open the body again by throwing in a handful of oat-meal; by this means they expedite their work but at the same time they leave it quite grainy from the want of labour. This, in handling the dry grey hat when made, may be in part discovered. The beaver for the nap is laid on towards the conclusion of this kind of working. The hat now possesses the form of a cone, and the whole of the several actions it has undergone have converted it into a soft flexible felt, capable of being extended, though with some difficulty, in any or every direction; therefore the next thing to be done, is to give it the form required by the wearer. For this purpose, the workman turns up the edge of brim to the depth of about an inch and a half, and then returns the point back again through the centre or axis of the cap, so far as not to take out this fold, but to produce another inner fold of the same depth. The point being returned back again in the same manner, produces a third fold, and thus the workman proceeds until the whole has acquired the appearance of a flat circular piece, consisting of a number of concentric undulations, rings, or folds, with the point in the centre. This is laid upon the plank, where the workman, keeping it wet with the liquor, pulls out the point with his fingers, and presses it down with his hand, at the same time turning it round on its centre in contact with the plank, till he has, by this means rubbed out a flat portion equal to the intended crown of the hat. In the next place, he takes a block, to the crown of which he applies the flat central portion of the felt, and by forcing a string down the sides of the block, causes the next part to assume the figure of the crown, which he continues to wet and work until it has properly disposed itself round the block. The brim now appears like a flounced or puckered appendage round the edge of the crown; but the block being set upright on the plank, the requisite figure is soon given by working rubbing, and extending this part. Water only is used in this operation of fashioning or blocking; at the conclusion of which it is pressed out by the blunt edge of a copper implement used for that purpose called a *stamper*.

Previous to the dying, the nap of the hat is raised or loosened out with a wire-brush, or carding instrument. The fibres are too rotten after the dying to bear this operation. The dying materials are logwood, a little oak-bark, and a mixture of the sulphats of iron and of copper, known in the market by the common names of green copperas and blue vitriol. The hats are boiled with logwood, and afterwards immersed in the saline solution. The dyed hats are, in the next place taken to the stiffening-shop. One workman, assisted by a boy, does this part of the business. He has two vessels, or boilers, one containing the grounds of strong beer, and the other containing melted glue, a little thinner than what is used by carpenters. The beer-grounds are applied in the inside of the crown to prevent the glue from coming through to the face, and also to give the requisite firmness at a less expence than could be produced by glue alone. Were the glue to pass through the hat in different places, it would be more difficult to produce an even gloss upon the face in the subsequent finishing. The glue is therefore applied after the beer-grounds are dried, and then only upon the lower face of the brim, and the inside of the crown. For this purpose, the hat is put into another hat, called a stiffening hat, the crown of which is notched, or slit, open in various directions. These are then placed in a hole in a dealboard, which supports the brim, and the glue is applied with a brush. In France, however, they use wine-lees instead of beer-grounds, and gum-water instead of glue.

The dry hat after this operation, is always rigid and its figure irregular. The last dressing is given by the application of moisture and heat, and the use of the brush, and a hot iron as before mentioned, somewhat in the shape of that used by tailors, but shorter and broader on the face. The hat being softened by exposure to steam, is drawn upon a block to which it is securely applied by the former method of forcing a string down from the crown to commencement of the brim. The judgement of the workman, is employed in moistening, brushing, and ironing the hat, in order to give and preserve the proper figure. When the brim of the hat is not intended to be of an equal width throughout, as is oftentimes the case for military hats, it is cut by means of a wooden or metallic pattern. The contrivance for cutting them round, is very ingenious and simple. A number of notches are made in one edge of a flat piece of wood, for the purpose of inserting the point of a knife, and from one side or edge of this piece of wood, there proceeds a straight handle, which lies parallel to the notched side, forming an angle somewhat like that of a carpenter's square. When the legs of this angle are applied to the outside of the crown, and the board lies flat on the brim of the hat, the notched edge will lie nearly in the direction of the radius, or line pointing to the centre of the hat. A knife being therefore inserted in one of the notches, it is easy to draw it round by leaning the tool against the crown, and it will cut the brim very regular and true. This cut is made before the hat is quite finished, and is not carried entirely through; so that one of the last operations consist in tearing off the redundant part, which by that means leaves an edging of beaver round the external face of the brim. When the hat is completely finished, the crown is tied up in gauze paper, which is neatly ironed down. It is then ready for the subsequent operations of lining &c. for sale.

THE JEWELLER

It appears from history that the profession of a jeweller is of very antient date; for we read in the Bible that Aaron had a breast-plate set with a variety of precious stones: and in succeeding ages there is a frequent mention of rings and other ornaments being made of gold and set with stones. Hence the name jeweller, one who sets jewels, or precious stones, is properly derived. There is scarcely a nation in the world who have not employed jewellers of some kind or other. When Captain Cook visited the South Sea islands, where, perhaps, no civilized being had been before, they found the natives with their ears, noses, and arms, ornamented with pearls, gold, shells, and curious teeth of fish, in a fanciful manner.

Civilized countries have greatly improved the art of jewellery. The French for lightness and elegance of design have surpassed their neighbours; but the English jewellers, for excellence of workmanship, have been, and still are, superior to every other nation. The name jeweller is now commonly applied to all who set stones, whether real or artificial; but, properly speaking, it belongs only to those who set diamonds and other precious gems. According to the general application of the term, jewellers make rings of all sorts in gold, lockets, bracelets, broaches, ornaments for the head, ear-rings, necklaces, and a great variety of trinkets composed of *diamonds, pearls*, or other stones.

The DIAMOND was called by the antients *adamant*; as a precious stone, it holds the first rank, in value, hardness, and lustre of all gems. The goodness of diamonds consists in their *water*, or colour, lustre and weight. The most perfect colour is the white. The defects in diamonds are veins, flaws, specks of red and black sand, and a blueish or yellowish cast.

In Europe, lapidaries examine the goodness of their diamonds by daylight, but in the Indies they do it by night: for the purpose, a hole is made in the wall, where a lamp is placed, with a thick wick, by the light of which they judge of the goodness of the stone.

Diamonds are found in the East Indies, principally in the kingdoms of Golconda, Visapour, Bengal, and the island of Borneo. They are obtained from mines and rivers.

As the diamond is the hardest of all precious stones, it can only be cut and ground by itself and its own substance. To bring diamonds to that degree of perfection which augments their price so considerably, the workmen rub several against each other; and the powder, thus rubbed off the stones, and received in a little box for the purpose, serves to grind and polish others.

The PEARL is a hard, white, smooth shining body, found in shell-fish resembling an oyster, and is ranked among the gems. The perfection of pearls, whatever be their shape, consists chiefly in the lustre and clearness of their colour, which jewellers call their water. Those which are white are the most esteemed in Europe; while many Indians and the Arabs prefer the yellow: some are of a lead colour, some border on the black and some are quite black. The *oriental* pearls are the finest on account of their largeness, colour, and beauty, being generally of a beautiful silver white; those found in the western hemisphere are more of a milk-white.

In Europe *pearls* and *diamonds* are sold by *carat* weight, the carat being equal to four grains; but in Asia, the weights made use of are different in different states.

Leathern skins are fastened to the board at which the jeweller works, to catch the filings and small pieces of precious metals, which would otherwise be liable to fall on the ground. The tools used are files of various kinds, and drills; beside a small hammer, a pair of pliers, and, on a little block of wood, a small crucible. A *drill bow* is also used; this is a flexible instrument, consisting of a piece of steel, to the ends of which is fastened a cat-gut: the cat-gut is twisted round one of the drills and then it is fitted for the business.

Behind the jeweller is fixed a drawing-bench, on which he draws out his wire to any degree of fineness. The method of drawing wire from gold or other metals is this: The metal is first made into a cylindric form; when it is drawn through holes of several irons, each smaller than the other, till it is as fine as it is wanted, sometimes much smaller than a hair. Every new hole lessens its diameter: but it gains in length what it loses in thickness; a single ounce is frequently drawn to a length of several thousand feet.

The jeweller's crucible will be heated in a *forge* which is an essential article in a jewellers's shop. Another very material tool is the anvil and block.

A *flatting-mill* is also wanted, and indeed cannot be dispensed with where the business is considerable. The flatting-mill consists of two perfectly round and very highly polished rollers, formed internally of iron, and welded over with a plate of refined steel; the circumference of these rollers nearly touch each other; they are both turned with one handle. The lowermost roller is about ten inches in diameter, and the upper one is much smaller. The wire that is to be flattened, unwinding from a bobbin, and passing through a narrow slit in an upright piece of wood, called a *ketch*, is directed by a small conical hole in a piece of iron, called a *guide*, to any particular width of the rollers; some of which, by means of this contrivance, are capable of receiving forty threads.

After the wire is flatted it is again wound on a bobbin, which is turned by a wheel, fixed on the axis of one of the rolls, and so managed that the motion of the bobbin just keeps pace with that of the rolls.

Besides those which are already mentioned, jewellers require a great variety of other tools; such as *gravers, scorpers, spit-stickers, knife-tools, straining-weights, brass-stamps, lamp and blow-pipe, ring sizes, spring-tongues, piercing-saws, boiling-pans, shears,* &c. &c.

The trade of a jeweller has always been considerable in London; but, like many others, it is very much affected by a war, and at this moment is exceedingly flat, During the American war, thousands of that business were almost in a starving condition: those only who are capable of turning their genius to other mechanical pursuits are likely to obtain employment at such times.

Some jewellers will earn as journey-men four guineas a week: but the general run of wages is about 25 or 30 shilings.

THE BRICKLAYER

Structures of brick as we now see them, are by no means of so old a date as may probably be supposed. Bricks indeed were much used by the Romans, though of a different size and shape to those of our own time. Instances of them may be particularly seen in the walls of Old Verulam, in the castle of Colchester, and in different parts of the abbey church of St. Albans, which was built in the Saxon times out of the ruins of the Roman city.

Bricks appear to have been again introduced in one or two instances as early as the reign of Richard the Third: though few buildings of consequence were erected with them before the reign of Henry the Sixth. Some of the oldest and best specimens now remaining may be found in the remains of Hurtsmonceaux castle in Sussex, and the gate of the Rye-house in Hertfordshire, both built very early in the reign of Henry the Sixth; the Lollards tower at Lambeth Palace built in 1454; Dandelion gateway of the time of Henry the Seventh; and the old part of Hampton-court, built in 1514, by Cardinal Wolsey.

The bricklayer is an artificer who builds walls, &c. with bricks. In London this business includes tyling, walling, chimney-work, and paving with bricks and tiles. Tylers and bricklayers were incorporated, by Elizabeth, under the name of masters and wardens of the society of freemen of the mystery and art of tylers and bricklayers. In the country, plaisterers' work is always joined to the business of bricklayer, and not unfrequently stone-mason's work also.

The materials made use of by bricklayers are bricks, tiles, mortar, laths, nails, and tile-pins.

Their tools are a brick-trowel, to take up and spread the mortar; a brick-axe, to cut bricks to the proper shape and size; a saw is also occasionally wanted, and a stone to rub the bricks smooth when great exactness is required. A square is always wanted to lay the bed or foundation of any wall or building; a bevel, with which the undersides of the bricks are cut to a required angle; a piece of timber, called a *banker* — this is about six feet long, and laid on two other piers of timber, three feet high from the floor on which they stand, and on this they cut the bricks. Line-pins and a line are used to lay the courses or rows of bricks by; a plumb-rule, by which they carry their work up-right. A level is wanted to conduct the building exactly horizontal; a small square to set off right angles; a ten foot rod to take dimensions; and a jointer, or long flat lath about three inches wide, which is held by two men, while another draws the long joints; a rammer, to render the foundation firm, by beating or ramming; a crowe, pick-axe, and shovel, with which they dig through and clear away any obstacles that may oppose their progress.

Bricklayers are supplied with bricks and mortar by a man they call a *labourer*, who is also employed in making the mortar from lime. The labourer brings the mortar, and the bricks in a machine called a hod, which he carries on his shoulder. Before he puts the mortar into the hod, he throws over every part of the inner surface fine dry sand to prevent it from sticking to the wood.

A bricklayer and his labourer will lay in a single day about a thousand bricks, in what is called whole and solid work, when the wall is either a brick and a half or two bricks thick; and since a cubic yard contains 460 bricks, he will lay above two cubic yards in a day.

The wages of a journeyman bricklayer are from four shillings to five shillings and sixpence a day; the wages of a labourer, from half-a-crown to three shillings and sixpence a day.

The bricklayer's trowel is made of steel and of so much importance is this instrument in the arts of life, that the inventor of a new hammer, by which trowels are better and more expeditiously made, has lately received forty guineas, from the *Society of Arts, Manufacturers, &c.* in the Adelphi. The superior merit of trowels made by this hammer consists in their great elasticity, by which they always instantly return to the original shape although ever so much bent out of it. The bricklayer's scaffold consists of upright poles to which two or more horizontal ones are tied at one end, having the other fixed in the wall; and on the flat boards are laid.

Bricklayers compute new work, such as the walls of houses, &c. by the rod of 16½ feet, and the price charged includes the putting up and use of scaffolding; but the clearing out and carrying away the rubbish is equally an extra charge. In digging and steening of wells, the work is charged at a certain price per foot, and the price is higher for each foot according as the depth is greater.

The emptying and carrying away soil, that is to be removed for making foundations of vaults, is charged by the ton: eighteen cubic feet of soil is reckoned to weigh a ton.

THE CARPENTER

THERE is no art more useful than that which is exercised by the carpenter. It is his business to cut, fashion, and join timber and other wood for the purpose of building .

There are two kinds of carpenters: house-carpenters, and ship-carpenters: the term is however usually applied to those who perform the rough work in the building of houses; such as hewing out, and putting in their places, the beams, rafters, joists, &c: and those who do the lighter kind of work, as the making of doors, wainscoting and sashes, are called joiners: most of those, however, who are brought up to the trade are both carpenters and joiners.

The wood which they principally make use of is deal, oak, elm, and mahogany.

Deal is the wood of the fir-tree, which is chiefly brought from Sweden, Norway, and other northern European countries. The most common species of fir-trees are the *silver-leafed* and the *pitch, Norway,* or *spruce* fir. The first of these grows in many parts of Germany, from whence turpentine is sent into England; but the most beautiful are those that grow on mount Olympus. The Norway fir produces the white deal commonly used by carpenters; from this pitch is also drawn; when it takes its second name of the *pitch fir.*

Oak is too well known in this country to need any description; it is chiefly used by ship-builders, of whom we shall speak hereafter.

Mahogany is a species of cedar: it is a native of the warmer parts of America, growing plentifully in the islands of Cuba, Jamaica, and Domingo. In some instances these trees grow to so large a size as to be capable of being cut into planks of six feet in breadth; they rise to immense heights, notwithstanding they are sometimes found growing on rocks where there is scarcely any depth of earth.

The carpenter stands in need of a great variety of tools, such as saws, planes, chisels, hammers, awls, gimlets, &c. Common workmen are obliged to find their own tools, a set of which is worth from ten to twenty pounds, or even more. But for different kinds of mouldings, for beads, and fancy work, the master carpenter supplies his men with the necessary implements.

The practices in the art of carpentry and joinery are called planing, sawing, mortising, scribing, moulding, &c. The great difference in the trades of a carpenter, and a joiner, is that the former is employed in the larger, stronger, and coarser operations, and the latter in the smaller and more curious works.

Let us visualise the carpenter in the act of planing the edge of a board, that is held to the side of the bench by means of a screw which is always attached to it. On his bench are a hammer, pincers, mallet, and two chisels; a box also containing the turkey stone with which he sharpens his tools: the shavings taken off by his plane are scattered on his bench and on the ground: at the right hand corner stand some boards, and his bag in which he carries his tools: on the other side is the saw, upon the four-edged stool which he uses for various purposes. Behind him is a new door, some other boards, a saw hanging against the wall, and a basket in which he puts his smaller tools.

He is preparing boards, to lay upon the roof of a new house. The rafters are already in their place: the boards are to be laid next, in order to receive the slates.

The art of *sawing,* and the different kinds of saws made use of, will be described when we come to speak of the sawyer.

A *mortise* is a kind of joint, in which a hole of a certain depth is made in the thickness of a piece of wood, in order to receive another piece called a tenon.

Scribing is a term made use of when one side of a piece of stuff is to be fitted to the side of some other piece which is not regular.

To make the two join close together all the way, the carpenter *scribes* it; that is, he lays the piece of stuff to be *scribed* close to the other piece he intends to *scribe* to, and opens his compasses to the greatest distance the two pieces any where stand from each other; then bearing one of the legs against the side to be scribed to, with the other leg he draws a line on the stuff to be scribed. Thus he gets a line on the irregular piece parallel to the edge of the regular one; and if by a saw, or other instrument, the wood be cut exactly to the line, when the two pieces are put together they will make a neat joint.

Planing consist of taking off, as occasion may require, all the rough edges from wood, boards, &c. A plane consists of a piece of box-wood, very smooth at the bottom, serving as a stock or shaft; in the middle of which is an aperture for a steel edge, or very sharp chisel, to pass. This edge is easily adjusted by a stroke of the hammer at one of the ends of the stock.

Planes have different names, according to their forms, sizes, and uses; as the *Jack-plane*, which is about eighteen inches long and intended for the roughest kind of work.

The *long-plane* is two feet in length; it smooths the work after the rough stuff is taken off; it is well adapted for smoothing the edges of boards that are to be joined.

The *smoothing-plane* is only six or seven inches long, and is used on almost all occasions.

The *rabbet-plane* cuts the upper edge, of a board straight or square, down into the stuff, so that the edge of another, cut after the same manner may join with it on the square.

Besides these there are *plowing-planes, moulding-planes, hollow-planes, snipe's-bill planes,* &c.

Glue is a very important article in the carpenter's and joiner's trade. It is made of the skins of all kinds of beasts, reduced to the state of jelly: the older the animal the better is the glue that is made of its hide.

A ship-carpenter is an officer at sea, whose business consists in having things in readiness for keeping the vessel in which he is stationed, in repair attending to the stopping of leaks, to caulking, careening and the like. He is to watch the timber of the vessel, to see that it does not rot; and in time of battle he is to have every thing prepared for repairing and stopping breaches made by the enemy's cannon.

A journeyman carpenter, when he works by time, receives from three shillings and sixpence to four shillings and sixpence a day.

THE COOPER

A cooper manufactures casks, tubs of all sizes, pails, and sundry other articles useful in domestic concerns. These are made with oak timber, a great part of which comes from America, cut up into narrow pieces called staves; they are sometimes bent, and for other sorts of work they are straight. For tubs, pails, &c. the bottoms of which are less than the tops, the staves are wider at top than they are at the bottom. After the staves are dressed and ready to be arranged, the cooper without attempting any great nicety in sloping or bevilling them, so that the *whole* surface of the edge may touch in every point, brings them into contact only at the inner surface, and then by drawing the hoops *hard* (tight) he can make a closer joint than could be done by sloping the stave from the outer to the inner side. These staves are kept together by means of hoops, which are made of hazel and ash; but some articles require iron hoops. To make them hold water or other liquids, the cooper places between each stave from top to bottom split flags, which swell with moisture, and effectually prevent the vessel from leaking.

The coopers derive large profits and a great part of their employment from the West India trade. The puncheons and hogsheads, are used in the voyage out to the Island, for packing coarse goods, as coarse woollen cloths, coarse hats, &c. whence those vessels return filled with rum and sugar.

The tools required by the cooper are numerous, some of which are peculiar to his art; but most of them are common both to him and the carpenter.

In making a hogshead, the cooper holds, in his left hand, a flat piece of wood, which he lays on the edge of the hoop, while he strikes it with the hammer in his right hand. To make the hoops stick, he takes the precaution to chalk the staves before he begins this part of the operation. The tops and bottoms he puts together by means of wooden pegs.

The cooper uses various tools such as saws, axes, spoke-shaves, stocks and bits, adzes, augers &c. The structure and uses of the saw and the axe are too well known to stand in need of description.

Spoke-shaves are of different kinds; they are intended for uses similar to those for which the carpenter adapts his planes.

The *stock-and-bit* make but one instrument. The *stock* in the handle, and *the bit* is a sort of piercer that fits into the bottom of the stock: bits of various sorts are adapted to the same stock; of course, the bit is always moveable, and may instantly be replaced by one of a different bore.

An *adze* is a cutting tool of the axe kind, having its blade made very thin and arching: it is used chiefly for taking off thin chips, and for cutting the hollow side of boards, &c.

Augers, or, as they are sometimes spelt, *awgres*, are used for boring large holes: they are a kind of large gimlet, consisting of a wooden handle, and an iron blade which is terminated with a steel-bit.

The trade of the cooper was formerly among the cries of London; "Any work for the cooper?" is now heard in many parts of the country. A travelling cooper carries with him a few hoops of different sizes, some iron rivets, and wooden pegs, his hammer, adze, and stock-and-bit. With these few instruments he can repair all washing and brewing utensils, besides the churns and wooden vessels made use of in dairies. An ingenious working cooper will in his peregrinations readily perform sundry jobs that belong to the carpenter, in villages which are too small to support a person in that trade. A journeyman cooper, who works for a master, will earn from three to five shillings per day.

Every custom-house and excise-office has an officer called the *king's cooper*; and every large ship has a cooper on board, whose business is to look after all the casks intended for water, beer, and spirits.

This trade has to boast of a considerable antiquity; the operations of the cooper are referred to, 2000 years ago by the Roman writers on rural ecomony.

THE STONE-MASON

The business of the stone-mason consists in the art of hewing or squaring stones and marble; in cutting them for the purposes of building, and in being able to work them up with mortar.

When the stones are large, the business of hewing and cutting them belongs to the *stone-cutter;* but these are frequently ranked with the masons, and so also are those who fashion the ornaments of sculpture, though they are properly carvers and sculptors in stone.

The tools principally used by masons are the square, level, plumb-line, bevel, compass, hammer, chisel, mallet, saw, and trowel, besides these used by the hand the master mason ought to possess powerful machines for raising or rearing large stone, or other great burdens, as levers pullies, the wheel and axis, crane, &c.

When masons or bricklayers speak of a *bevel* angle they mean one which is neither forty-five or ninety degrees.

The stone-mason's saw is different from those used by other mechanics; it has no teeth; and being moved backwards and forwards by a single man, it cuts the stone by its own weight. In winter time, and in rainy or very sultry weather, the sawer sits in a wooden box, not unlike a watchman's box, but without a front to it. These boxes are moveable, so that the workman may secure himself from the piercing blasts of winter, and the scorching sun-beam in summer.

Both marble and stone are dug out of quarries: the grain of marble is so fine as readily to take a beautiful polish. It is of course much used in ornaments of building, as columns, statues, altars, tombs, chimney-pieces, tables, &c.

There are an indefinite number of different kinds of marbles, and they take their name either from their colour, their age, their country, their degree of hardness, or their defects. Some are of one colour only, as black or white; others are streaked, or varigated with stains, clouds, and veins; but almost all are opake, excepting the white, which when cut into very thin slices and polished becomes transparent.

Marble is polished by being first rubbed with free-stone, afterwards with pumice-stone, and lastly with emery or calcined tin. Artificial marble is real marble pulverized and mixed with plaster; and from this compostion are made statues, busts, basso-relievos, and other ornaments of architecture.

Few natural substances are less understood than marble: the people who are accustomed to work them, know from experience, and at first sight, that one sort will receive a high polish, that another is easily wrought, and a third refuses the tools. And men of science know little more.

Masons make use of several kinds of stone, but *Portland-stone* is the principal: of this there are vast quarries in the island of Portland in Dorsetshire, from whence it is brought in large quantities to London. It is used for building in general; for copings at the tops of houses, and as supports for iron rails; for windowcills; for stone balusters; for steps and paving where great neatness is required.

This stone is very soft when it comes out of the quarry; it works easily and becomes hard by length of time. The piers and arches of Westminster bridge are built with it; and so is the magnificent cathedral of St. Paul's.

Purbeck-stone comes from an island of that name also in Dorsetshire; it is chiefly used in paving, making steps, and other rough-work.

Yorkshire-stone is also used for paving, steps, coping, and other purposes in which strength and durability are required. There is also a stone which, when cut into slabs, is used for harths, called *Ryegate-stone.*

Stone-masons make use of *mortar, plaster of Paris,* and *tarrass,* for cementing or joining their works. The two former are used in dry work, and the latter for bridges and buildings exposed to the water.

Mortar is the composition of lime and sand mixed to a proper consistency with water.

Plaister of Paris is made by burning a stone called gypsum.

Tarras is a coarse sort of plaster, or mortar, durable in wet: it is chiefly used to line basons, cisterns, wells, and other reservoirs of water. That which is called Dutch tarrass is made of a soft rock-stone, found near Cologne on the Rhine: it is burnt like lime, and reduced to powder by mills, and from thence carried to Holland, by which means it has acquired the name of *Dutch* tarrass. It is very dear, on account of the great demand there is for its aquatic works.

An artificial tarrass is formed of two parts of lime and one of plaster of Paris; and another consists of one part of lime and two parts of well sifted coal ashes. These are all used occasionally by the mason and bricklayer.

Stone-masons measure and charge their work either by the superficial or cubic foot: they have extra charges for iron cramps, which fasten two or more stones together; for cutting holes in which iron rails are fixed, and for various other things.

The journeyman mason has about 4s or 4s 6d per day, and the labourer from 2s 6d to 3s per day; but others who work by the piece, or who are employed in carving or other fine work, will earn more than double that sum.

THE SAWYER

In the early periods of the world, the trunks of trees were split with wedges into as thin pieces as possible by that mode; and if it were necessary to have them still thinner, they were hewn on both sides by hatchets, till they were reduced to a proper size. The common saw, which requires only to be guided by the hand of the workman, was not known in America when it was discovered and subjugated by Europeans.

The saw is, undoubtedly, one of the most useful instruments in the mechanic arts, ever invented. Among the Greeks, the inventor has been enrolled in their mythology with a place among the gods, and honoured as one of the greatest benefactors of the human race. The invention is attributed to Icarus, the son of Daedalus, who is said to have taken the first hint from the spine or backbone of a flat-fish.

The best *saws* are of tempered steel, ground bright and polished: the edge, in which the teeth are, is always thicker than the back. The teeth are cut and sharpened by a triangular file. When filed, the teeth are to be *set* , that is, turned askew, or out of a right line, to make the fissure wider, that the back may follow with ease. This is done by putting an instrument between every two teeth, and giving it a little wrench, which turns one of the teeth in one direction, and the other in a contrary one.

The teeth are always set *ranker* for coarse cheap work, than for that which is hard and fine.

The *pit-saw* is a large two handed saw used to saw timber in pits. It is set rank for coarse stuff, so as to make a fissure of almost a quarter of an inch.

The sawyer cuts the trunks of trees into beams and planks, fit for the use of carpenters. The timber is laid on a frame over an oblong pit, called, a saw-pit, and it is cut by means of a long saw fastened in a frame, which is worked up and down by two men, one standing on the wood to be cut, and the other in the pit. As they proceed in their work, they drive wedges at a proper distance from the saw, to keep the fissure open, which enables the saw to move with freedom.

This is a very laborious employment, yet two industrious men may earn from twelve to eighteen shillings a day.

That the saws of the Grecian carpenters were of a similar form to the common pit saw now in use, is manifest from a painting preserved among the antiquities of Herculaneum. In this, the piece of wood to be sawn is secured by cramps. The saw consists of a square frame, having in the middle a blade. The piece of wood extends beyond the end of the bench, one of the workmen appears standing and the other sitting on the ground. The pit used in modern times is a great improvement, as the power of a man standing in the pit, must far exceed that exerted by him in a sitting posture.

The most beneficial and ingenious improvement of this instrument was the invention of *saw-mills*, which are worked either by water, by wind, or by steam. A saw-mill consists of several parallel saws, which are made to rise and fall perpendicularly by means of a mechanical motion. A very few hands are necessary to conduct this operation, to push forward the pieces of timber, which are either laid on rollers, or suspended by ropes, in proportion as the sawing advances.

But the sawing machines worked by steam in the *block-house* in Portsmouth dock-yard, convey to the spectator the nature of mechanical operations in the completest manner possible. The manufacture of blocks in that place cannot fail to interest every one who has the slightest turn for mechanics, and a person must be devoid of all curiosity, who can visit Portsmouth, and return without making every effort to be introduced into this part of the dock-yard.

THE SMITH

A Smith is one who works on iron, and who from that metal manufactures a vast variety of articles useful in the arts of life, and of great importance to domestic comfort. There are several branches in this trade: some are called *black-smiths* others are called *white-smiths*, or *bright-smiths*; these polish their work to a considerable degree of nicety; some include in their business bell-hanging, which is now carried to great perfection; others are chiefly employed in the manufacture of locks and keys.

In the smith's shop there must be a forge, an anvil and block, a vice fastened to an immovable bench, besides hammers, tongues, files, punches, and pincers, of different sorts.

The *forge* is the most prominent article, it is a sort of furnace intended for heating metals so hot as to render them malleable, and fit to be formed into various shapes. The back of the forge is built upright to the ceiling, and is enclosed over the fire-place with a *hovel* which leads into the chimney to carry away the smoke. In the back of the forge, against the fire-place, is a thick iron plate with a pipe fixed to it to receive the nose of the bellows. The bellows are behind the forge; these are worked by means of a *rocker*, with a string or chain fastened to it, which the smith or his labourer pulls. One of the boards of the bellows is fixed, and by drawing down the handle of the rocker the moveable board, which is also the upper one, rises, and by means of a weight on the top sinks again; and by this alternate motion the fire is raised to any degree of heat.

In front of the forge, but a little below it, is a *trough of water,* which is useful for wetting the coals to make them throw out a greater heat; the water serves also for cooling the tongs, with which the smith holds the heated iron, and which in a short time become too hot for him to grasp: in this trough also, the smith hardens his iron by dipping it while red-hot.

Iron is hammered or forged two ways; either by the force of the hand, in which there are sometimes several persons employed, one holding and turning the iron, and hammering likewise, while the others hammer only, with what are called sledge hammers; or it is done by the force of a water-mill, which raises and works several enormous hammers; under the stroke of these the men have only to present the large lumps of iron, which are sustained at one end by the anvils, and at the other by iron chains fastened to the ceiling of the forge. This last method is employed in the largest works, such as the making of anchors of ships, which weigh several thousand pounds.

In lighter works, such as in the making of stoves, shovels, gridirons, trivets, &c. &c. — a single man is sufficient to hold, to heat, and to turn the iron with one hand, while he strikes it with the other.

The several heats given by smiths to their iron are called the *blood-red* heat, the *white* heat, and the *welding* heat.

The blood-red heat is used when the iron has already acquired its form and size, but wants hammering only to smooth and fit it for the file.

The white heat is used when the iron has not its form and size, but must be forged into both.

The welding heat is required when two pieces of iron are to be united.

The uppermost surface of the *anvil,* on which a smith hammers his iron, must be very flat and smooth, and so hard that no file will touch it. At one end of the anvil is a hole, in which may be placed a strong steel chisel, or spike; on this a piece of red-hot iron may be laid, and cut in two with a single stroke of the hammer. Anvils are sometimes made of cast iron; but the best are those which are forged, with the upper part made of steel. The whole is usually mounted on a firm wooden block.

The *vice* fixed to the bench serves to hold any thing upon which the smith is at work, whether it requires filing, bending, or riveting, There are hand vices, and small anvils, which are occasionally used in the more delicate operations of this business.

Square and flat bars of iron are sometimes twisted for ornamental work; this is done by giving the metal a white heat, fixing it in the vice, and turning it with the tongs.

Iron rails before houses are generally made of cast iron which is run from the ore, and neither requires nor will bear the hammer; it is brittle, and will not yield in the least to the file. It is the business of the black-smith to make the upper rail to receive these bars, and to fix them into the stone-work.

It would be impossible to enumerate all the articles manufactured by the smith; they are of all kinds, and of almost all values. Steel stoves have been made especially at Brodie's manufactory in Carey-street, of several hundred pounds value; and a more interesting sight cannot well be viewed than the store-rooms of our large furnishing ironmongers.

Iron is dug out of the bowels of the earth in many parts of this kindom; and great quantities are imported from Sweden and North America, in pigs and bars.

Black-smiths charge for hammered work, such as rails, window bars &c. sixpence per lb; for ornamental work, as brackets, lamp-irons, &c. from fourteen to eighteen-pence per lb; about fifteen or eighteen shillings per hundred weight.

A journeymen smith will earn from three to five shillings per day; but those who work on the fine polished articles will earn much higher wages.

THE SHIP-WRIGHT

A Ship has been defined, a timber building, consisting of various parts and pieces, nailed and pinned together with iron and wood, in such form as to be fit to float, and to be conducted by wind and sails from sea to sea.

The word *ship* is a general name for all large vessels with sails, adapted for navigation on the sea; but by sailors the term is more particularly applied to a vessel furnished with three masts, each of which is composed of a lower-mast, a top-mast, and a top-gallant-mast.

The following observations we copy from Nicholson's Encyclopedia, and the improvement suggested is equally applicable to every other art. ''The man of science and the practical shipright have long lamented that, in the theory of the art of ship-building, an art so important in this country, there are so few fixed and posiiive principles established by demonstration or confirmed by practice; thus the artist being left to the exercise of his own opinion in general, resists theoretical propositions, however speciously formed, so hard has it ever been found to overcome habitual prejudice. The great neglect of the theory of ship-building is much to be deplored in a country like this, where the practical part is well understood and executed. Mathematics, engineering, and civil or house architecture are sciences nourished and taught in our universities and other schools; and to whatever degree of superiority scholars may arrive in those, shew them shipping draughts, or talk to them of the science of ship-building, and they appear as much at a loss as though they had never heard of such an art. This however is the picture of a few years ago, it is begun to be studied as a science under the denomination of *naval architecture;* for the promotion of this science, a very respectable body of ingenious men have for the last fifteen years associated.

In ship-building three things are necessary to be considered; first to give the vessel such a form as shall be best adapted for sailing, and for the service for which she is designed; secondly, to unite the several parts into a compact frame; and thirdly, to provide suitable accommodations for the officers and crew, as well as for the cargo, furniture, provisions, guns, and ammunition.

The outside figure of the ship includes the bottom or the hold, and the upper works which are also called the *dead works,* the first is that part which is generally under the water, the second are those which are usually above it, when the vessel is laden.

To give a proper shape to the bottom of the ship, it is necessary to consider the service for which she is designed, A *ship of war* should be able to sail swiftly, and carry her lower tier of guns four or five feet out of the water; a *merchant ship* ought to be able to contain a large cargo of goods, and to be navigated with few hands; both of these should be able to carry sail firmly: to steer well; and to sustain the shocks of the sea without being violently strained.

Ships are built principally with *oak* timber, which is the stoutest and strongest wood we have, and therefore, best fitted both to keep sound under water, and to bear the blows and shocks of the waves, and the terrible strokes of cannon-balls. For this last purpose, it is a peculiar excellence of the oak, that it is not so liable to splinter or shiver as other woods, so that a ball can pass through it without making a large hole. The great use of the oak for the structure of merchant-ships, as well as for men of war, is referred to by Mr. Pope:

While by our oaks the precious loads are borne,
And realms commanded which those trees adorn.

During the construction of a ship, she is supported in the dock, or upon a wharf, by a number of solid blocks of timber placed at equal distances from and parallel to each other, in which situation she is said to be *on the stocks*.

The first piece of timber laid upon the blocks is generally the *keel*, which, at one end, is let into the stern-post, and at the other into the *stem*. If the carcase of a ship be compared to the skeleton of a human body, the *keel* may be considered as the back-bone, and the timbers as the ribs.

The *stern* is the hinder part of the ship, near which are the state-room, cabins, &c. To the stern post is fixed the iron-work that holds the *rudder*, which directs the course of the vessel.

The *stem* is a circular piece of timber in the front; into this the sides of the ship are inserted. The outside of the stem is usually marked with a scale or division of feet, according to its perpendicular height from the keep; the intention of this is to ascertain the draught of water at the fore-part, when the ship is in preparation for a sea voyage.

The ship-wright stands on a scaffold at the stern, and drives in the wedges with his wooden trunnel. The holes are first bored with the auger, and then the wedges drove in; these are afterwards cut off with a saw.

The *caulking* of a ship is a very important operation; it consists in driving *oakum,* (or old ropes untwisted, and the substance pulled into loose hemp) into the seams of the planks, to prevent the ship's leaking. It is afterwards covered with hot melted pitch or rosin, to prevent it rotting.

A mixture was formerly used for covering the bottom of ships, made of one part of tallow, one of brimstone, and three of rosin; this is called paying the bottom. The sides and bottom are usually *payed* with coal tar, the produce of England.

To enable ships to sail well, the outsides in contact with the water are frequently covered with copper.

The masts of ships are made of *fir* or *pine,* on account of the straightness and lightness of that wood; the length of the *main-mast* of an East India ship is about eighty feet. The masts always bear a certain proportion to the breadth of the ship; whatever the breadth may be, multiply that by twelve, and divide the product by five, which gives the *length* of the *main-mast*. Thus, a ship which measures thirty feet at the broadest part will have a main-mast seventy-two feet long; the thickness of the mast is estimated by allowing one inch for every three feet in length, accordingly, a mast seventy-two feet long must be twenty-four inches thick. For the other masts different proportions are to be used. To the masts are attached the yards, sails, and rigging; which receive the wind necessary for navigation.

In a dock-yard where ships are built, six or eight men, called *quartermen*, are frequently intrusted to build a ship, and engage to perform the business for a certain sum, under the inspection of a master builder. These employ other men under them, who according to their different departments, will earn from fifteen or twenty shillings to two or three pounds per week.

When a ship is finished building, it is to be *launched,* that is, put out of dock. To render the operation of launching easy the ship when first built is supported by two strong platforms laid with gradual inclination to the water. Upon the surface of this declivity are placed two corresponding ranges of planks, which compose the base of the frame, called the *cradle,* to which the ship's bottom is securely attached. The planes of the cradle and platform are well greased, and the *blocks* and *wedges,* by which the ship was supported, are driven out from under the keel; afterwards the *shores,* by which she is retained on the stocks, are cut away, and the ship slides down into the water.

Ships of the first rate are usually constructed in dry docks, and afterwards floated out, by throwing open the flood-gates, and suffering the tide to enter, as soon as they are finished.

THE MARINER

A mariner is in common language the same as sailor or seaman. Mariners are sometimes employed on board merchant ships, and sometimes in men of war. In merchants' employ, the mariners are accountable to the master, the master to the owners of the vessel, and the owners to the merchant, for any damages that may happen. If a vessel is lost by tempest, the mariners lose their wages, and the owners their freight: this is intended to make them use their utmost endeavours to preserve the ship committed to their care.

Mariners on board the king's ships are subject to strict regulations, which however, depend on certain fixed laws passed at different times by parliament. Mariners who are not in his Majesty's service are liable during the time of war to be impressed, unless they enter voluntarily, to which they are encouraged by bounties and high wages: and every foreign seaman, who, during war, shall serve two years in any man of war, merchantman, or privateer, become naturalized.

The mariner of higher rank understands the art of navigation, or of conducting a vessel from one place to another, in the safest, shortest, and most commodious way. He ought therefore to be well acquainted with the islands, rocks, sands, and straights, near which he has to sail. He should also know the signs which indicate the approach to land; these, are the appearing of birds; the floating of weeds on the surface of the sea: the depth and colour of the sea. He should, moreover, understand the nature of the winds, particularly the times when the *trade* winds and monsoons set in; the seasons when storms and hurricanes may be expected, and the signs of their approach; the motion of currents and of tides. He must understand also the working of a ship; that is, the management of the sails, rigging, &c.

Navigation or the proper employment of the mariner, is either *common* or *proper*. The former is usually called coasting; that is, where the ships are on the same, or very neighbouring coasts; and where the vessel is seldom out of sight of land, or out of reach of *sounding*. In this case, little more is required than an acquaintance with the lands they have to pass. the compass, and the sounding-line.

To gain a knowledge of the coast, a good chart or map is necessary.

The *compass,* or mariner's compass, as it is usually called, is intended to direct and ascertain a ship's course at sea. It consists of a circular brass box, which contains a card, with the thirty-two points of the compass fixed on a magnetic needle that always turns to the north, or nearly so. The needle with the card turns on an upright pin fixed in the centre of the box.

The top of the box is covered with glass, to prevent the wind from disturbing the motion of the card. The whole is inclosed in another box of wood, where it is suspended by brass hoops to keep the card in a horizontal position, whatever the motion of the ship may be; and it is so placed in the ship, that the middle section of the box may lie over the middle section of the ship along its keel.

The method of finding, by the compass, the direction in which a ship sails, is this: The compass being suspended, the mariner looks horizontally over it in the direction of the ship's *wake* (the wake of a ship is the print or tract impressed by the course of a ship on the surface of the water), by which he sees the point of the compass denoting the direction of the wake; the point opposite to this is that to which the ship is sailing according to the compass; and knowing how much the compass varies, he can tell the true point of the horizon to which he is going.

The *sounding-line* is a line with a plummet at the end: it is used to try the depth of the water and the quality of the bottom.

In *navigation proper,* which is where the voyage is long, and pursued through the main ocean, there are many other requisites wanted besides those already mentioned. Here a considerable skill in mathematics, and astronomy is required and an aptness in using instruments for celestial observations.

The *light-house* is erected on a rock, and having in the night a fire or other considerable light at the top, so as to be seen at a great distance from land. The use of the light-house is to direct the ships on the coast, to prevent them from running on the shore, and from other injuries by an improper course.

The wages of a mariner depend upon his employment, that is, whether he be in the King's service or on board a merchantman: they depend also upon the size of the ship, and upon the situation which he holds in it.

There is no profession of more importance to the interests of this country than that of the mariner. Government therefore provides, for those who are disabled, a place in Greenwich Hospital; and to the widows and children of those who are slain in defending their country, small pensions are granted. Greenwich Hospital is supported by the nation, and by sixpence a month deducted out of every seaman's wages.

The use of the compass we have as above; the following is the history of its discovery.

The magnet, or loadstone, was certainly known to the philosphers of ancient Greece for its quality of attracting iron; and, in later ages, the few who were in possession of the secret were enabled to perform tricks which the amazement of the ignorant ascribed to magic: but till about the end of the twelfth century we find no good authority to shew that its more valuable property, its polarity, or that power by which one point of it, or even of a needle or bar of iron touched with it, turns to the North pole, was known, at least in the western parts of the world.

Several authors, says Mr. Macpherson in his Annals of Commerce, strenuously assert that the Chinese have known the polarity of the magnet, and have had the use of the compass, a great many centuries before it was known in Europe. But they do not seem satisfactorily to prove their point, since after *asserting* that the compass was known, they fail in proving the knowledge of its most valuable use, in conducting a ship across the ocean.

About the conclusion of the twelfth century, says Mr. Macpherson, the earliest notice, I believe, that is to be found of the polarity of the magnet, and its use by seamen, appears in the Poetical Works of Hugues de Bercy, called also Guiot of Provins.

Jacebus de Vitriaco, also, who lived at the same time, and was Bishop of Acon in Palestine, writing on some of the natural productions of the East, mentions it under the name of Adamant, but at the same time describes it as indispensably necessary to all who use the sea.

In defiance, however, of these authorities, the Italian writers claim the honour of the invention for Flavio Gioia, a citizen of Amalfi on the coast of the Adriatic, who they say first used it in the year 1302 or 1320.

The truth, however, seems to be that the very early mariners to whom the use of the magnetic needle was familiar were accustomed to place it on a floating-straw: while the addition of a circular card, on which the different winds were represented, affixed to the needle and traversing with it, was apparently the improvement of Gioia. If other proofs were wanting to show that the invention was known long before the beginning of the thirteenth century, numerous writers might be quoted by whom its form and qualities are successively described. Peter Adsiger, whose letter dated in 1269, is said yet to remain in the library in the university of Leyden, not only wrote upon the various properties of the magnet, and the construction of the azimuth compass, but on the *variation* of the magnetic needle: a discovery, the credit of which was attributed first to Columbus in 1492, and afterwards to Sebastian Cabot in 1500, who seem only to have had greater opportunities than other people of remarking that the needle was not perfectly true to the north point, but diverged or varied a little from it.

The mariner's compass was long very rude and imperfect, but at length received great improvement from the invention and experiments of Dr. Knight, Mr. Smeaton and Mr. M'Culloch about the middle of the sixteenth century. So confident were some persons that the needle invariably pointed due north, that they treated with contempt the notion of the *variation,* which about that time began to be suspected. Careful observations however, soon discovered that in England and its neighbourhood the needle pointed to the eastward of the true north line; and the qauntity of this deviation being known, mariners continued to rely as firmly upon their compass, as if it had no so such irregularity, or by making an allowance for the due variation, the exact course could be readily obtained. From succeeding observations it was afterwards found that the deviation from the north was variable, that it gradually diminished, until in 1657 it pointed due north at London since then its has been veering to the westward.

From this short history of the discovery of the variation we may safely conclude the very great folly of ridiculing either dicovery or even the suspect of it; it is also much to be lamented that minds possessing activity enough to pursue enquiries to a certain extent, have not had strength enough to disregard ridicule or opposition, and follow the dictates of their own understandings. It was by firmness of pursuit that Columbus discovered America in defiance of his inveterate enemies, and that Arkwright completed his inventions, maugre the conflagration kindled by his affectionate help-mate; not to mention innumerable other instances of successful perseverance.

THE CURRIER

The business of the currier is to prepare hides, which have been under the hands of the tanner, for the use of shoemakers, coachmakers, saddlers, book-binders, &c.

Currying is the last preparation of leather, and puts it into a condition to be made up into shoes, saddles, harness, &c., it is performed two ways either upon the *flesh* or the *grain.*

In dressing leather for shoes *on the flesh,* the first operation is soaking the leather in water, until it be thoroughly wet; then the flesh side is shaved on a beam, that is, a sort of wooden block fixed on the ground to which the currier stands at his work, with a knife of a peculiar construction, and which indeed varies in different places; this is one of the most curious and laborious operations in the art of currying.

The knife used for this purpose is of a rectangular form, with two handles, one at each end, and a double edge. The best knives are said to be manufactured at Cirencester, and composed of iron and steel: the edge is made by rubbing them on a flat stone of a gritty substance till it comes to a kind of wire; the wire is taken off by a finer stone, and the edge is then turned to a kind of groovy wire by a piece of steel in form of a bodkin; this steel is used to renew the edge in the operation.

After the leather is properly shaved, it is thrown into water again, and scoured upon a board or stone appropriated to the use. Scouring is performed by rubbing the grain of hair side with a piece of pumice stone, or some other stone of a good grit, by which means a white sort of substance is forced out of the leather, called the *bloom,* produced in the operation of the tanning. The hide is then conveyed to the shade, or drying-place, when the oily substances are applied, which are put on both sides of the leather but in a greater and thicker quantity on the flesh, than on the hair, side. Thus far is the process of currying in its wet state, and thus far it is called *getting out.*

When the skin is quite dry, it undergoes other operations for the purpose of softening the leather. Whitening or paring succeeds, which is performed with a fine edge on the knife already described. It is then *boarded up,* or grained again, by applying the graining-board, first to the grain, and then to the flesh, side.

It is now fit for *waxing,* which is performed by rubbing it with a brush dipped in a composition of oil and lamp-black, on the flesh side, till it be thoroughly black: it is then *sized,* called black sizing, with a brush or sponge, dried and tallowed. After undergoing some other operations, this sort of leather, called waxed leather, is *curried.*

For leather curried on the hair side, termed black on the grain, the first operation is the same with that already described, till it is scoured. Then the black which is a solution of copperas in bark liquor, is applied to it while wet: this is first put upon the grain, after it has been rubbed over with a brush dipped in urine; and when it is dry it is *seasoned,* that is, rubbed over with a brush dipped in copperas water on the grain, till it be perfectly black: after this, the grain is raised with a fine graining board, and the leather is oiled with a mixture of oil and tallow, when it is finished, and fit for the shoe-maker.

Hides are sometimes *curried* for the use of saddlers and collar-makers, but the principal operations are much the same as those which have been already described. Hides for the roofs of coaches are shaved nearly as thin as those for shoes, and blacked on the grain.

In many places, the business of the currier connects with it that of the leather-dresser and leather-cutter, who supplies the shoe makers and others with all their leather, black, red, blue, green, &c.

Leadenhall-Market is one of the principal marts for leather: and shoe-makers, and leather-cutters in the country, who can command the capital, buy the greater part of their goods, particularly their sole-leather, there.

The curriers have been an incorporated company ever since the beginning of the reign of James the First; and during the reign of Queen Elizabeth, history records an account of a fierce contention between the curriers and shoe-makers, respecting the dressing of leather and the price to be paid them for their work; and also respecting the places in which leather should be sold. At length it was stipulated, in the year 1590, among other articles, that the curriers should have the dressing of all the leather brought into Leadenhall and Southwark Markets, and within three miles of London.

The use of skins is very ancient, the first garments in the world having been made of them. Moroccoes are made of the skins of a kind of goats. *Parchment* is made of sheep-skins. The true chamois leather is made of the skin of an animal of the same name, though it is frequently counterfeited with common goat's and sheep skin.

The Indian women in Carolina and Virginia dress buck and doe-skin with a considerable degree of skill; and so quick that a single woman will completely dress eight or ten skins in a day.

THE APOTHECARY

THE OFFICE of Apothecary is to attend on sick persons, and to prepare and give them medicines, either on his own judgement or according to the prescription of the physician.

It is well known that the word *apotheca* signified originally any kind of store, magazine, or warehouse; and that the proprietor or keeper of such a store was called *apothecarius*. We must not, therefore, understand by the word, when mentioned in writings two or three hundred years old, apothecaries such as ours are at present. At those periods, persons were often called apothecaries, who at courts, and in the houses of great people, prepared for the table various preserves, particularly fruit incrusted with sugar, and who on that account may be considered as confectioners. Hence, perhaps, we see the reason why apothecaries were in this country combined with the *grocers*, till the reign of James the First. They were then separated, and the apothecaries were incorporated as a company: the reason assigned for this was, that medicines might be better prepared, and that unwholesome remedies might not be imposed on the sick.

From this period, apothecaries were distinguished for selling drugs used in medicine, and preparing from them different compounds, according to the prescriptions given by physicians and others. Prior to this, it is probable, physicians usually prepared their own medicines; and it has been thought that they gradually became accustomed to employ apothecaries for the sake of their own convenience, when they found in their neighbourhood a druggist in whose skill they wished to promote, by resigning in his favour that part of the occupation.

Such an employment as that of an apothecary is, however, mentioned at a much earlier period of our history; for it is said, that King Edward the Third gave a pension of sixpence a day to Coursus de Gangeland, as apothecary, in London for taking care of and attending his majesty during his illness in Scotland; and this is the first mention of an apothecary.

In the year 1712 the importance of this profession was acknowledged by an act of parliament, which exempted for a limited time apothecaries from serving the offices of constables, and scavenger, and other ward and parish offices, and from serving upon juries; which act was a few years afterwards made perpetual.

The apothecaries, as a body, have a hall near Bridge-street, Black-friars, where there are two magnificent laboratories, out of which all the surgeons chests are supplied with medicines for the British navy. Here also things of all sorts are sold to the public, which may be depended upon as pure and unadulterated. They are obliged to make up their medicines according to the formulas prescibed in the college dispensary, and are liable to have their shops visited by censors of the college, who are employed to destroy such medicines as they think not good. But as almost all persons who practise in this profession are men of liberal education, and acquainted with the theory and practice of chemistry, there are very few of them who do not prepare their own drugs either wholly or in part.

In many places, and particularly in opulent cities, the first apothecaries' shops were established at the public expence, and belonged in fact to the magistrates. A particular garden also was often appropriated to the use of the apothecary, in order that he might rear in it the necessary plants, and which was therefore called the apothecaries' garden.

In conformity to this principle, Sir Hans Sloane, in the year 1721, presented the apothecaries' company with a spacious piece of ground at Chelsea, for a physic-garden, on condition of their paying the small ground rent of 5l. per annum; of continuing it always as a physic-garden, and of presenting to the Royal Society fifty samples of different sorts of plants grown there, till they amounted to two thousand. The latter of these conditions has been long since more than completed.

In this garden there are two very magnificent cedars, which were planted in 1683, and were then about three feet high. The pine-tree, coffee-tree, tea-shrub, and sugar-cane, are among the curiosities which may be seen at this place.

This is a very genteel business; a youth intended to be an apothecary should be a good scholar, at least he should know as much of Latin as to be able to read the best writers in the various sciences connected with medicine.

All persons apprenticed to an apothecary are bound for eight years. An assistant, or journeyman, to an apothecary will have from forty to fourscore pounds per annum, exclusive of his board.

In China they have a singular mode of dispensing their medicines. In the public squares of their cities, there is a very high stone pillar, on which are engraven the names of all sorts of medicines, with the price of each; and when the poor stand in need of such assistance, they go to the treasury, where they receive the price each medicine is rated at.

THE BAKER

The business of the Baker consists in making bread, rolls, and biscuits, and in baking various kinds of provisions.

It is not known when this very useful business first became a particular profession. Bakers were a distinct body of people in Rome nearly two hundred years before the Christian era, and it is supposed that they came from Greece. To these were added a number of freemen, who were incorporated into a *college* , from which neither they nor their children were allowed to withdraw. They held their effects in common, without enjoying any power of parting with them. Each bake-house had a *patron*, who had the superintendency of it; and one of the patrons had the management of the others, and the care of the college. So respectable were the bakers at Rome, that occasionally one of the body was admitted among the senators. Even by our own statutes the bakers are declared not to be handicrafts; and in London they are under the particular jurisdiction of the lord mayor and aldermen, who fix the price of bread, and have the power of fining those who do not conform to their rules.

Bread is made of flour mixed and kneaded with yeast, water, and a little salt. It is known in London under two names, the *white* or *wheaten*, and the *household*: these differ only in degrees of purity; and the loaves must be marked with a W. or H, or the baker is liable to suffer a penalty.

The process of bread-making is thus described:— To a peck of meal are added a handful of salt, a pint of yeast, and three quarts of water, cold in summer, hot in winter, and temperate between the two. The whole being kneaded, will rise in about an hour; it is then moulded into loaves, and put into the oven to bake.

The oven takes more than an hour to heat properly, and bread about three hours to bake. Most bakers make and sell rolls in the morning; these are either *common*, or *French* rolls: the former differ but little from loaf-bread: the ingredients of the latter are mixed with milk instead of water, and the finest flour is made use of for them. Rolls require only about twenty minutes for baking.

The life of a baker is very laborious; the greater part of his work being done by night: the journeyman is required always to commence his operations about eleven o'clock in the evening, in order to get the new bread ready for admitting the rolls in the morning. His wages are, however, but very moderate, seldom amounting to more than ten shillings a week, exclusive of his board.

The price of bread is regulated according to the price of wheat; and bakers are directed in this by the magistrates, whose rules they are bound to follow. By these the peck-loaf of each sort of bread must weigh seventeen pounds six ounces avoirdupois weight, and smaller loaves in the same proportion. Every sack of flour is to weigh two hundred and a half; and from this there ought to be made, at an average, twenty such peck-loaves, or eighty common quartern-loaves.

If bread were short in its weight only one ounce in thirty-six, the baker formerly was liable to be put in the pillory; and for the same offence he may now be fined, at the will of the magistrate, in any sum not less than one shilling, nor more than five shillings for every ounce wanting; such bread being complained of and weighed in the presence of the magistrate within twenty-four hours after it is baked, because bread loses in weight by keeping.

The process of biscuit-baking, as practised at the Victualling-office at Deptford, is curious and interesting. The dough, which consists of flour and water only, is worked by a large machine. It is then handed over to a second workman, who slices it with a large knife for the bakers, of whom there are five. The first, or the *moulder*, forms the biscuits two at a time; the second, or *marker*, stamps and throws them to the splitter, who separates the two pieces, and puts them under the hand of the chucker, the man that supplies the oven, whose work of throwing the bread on the peel must be so exact, that he cannot look off for a moment. The fifth, or the depositer, receives the biscuits on the peel, and arranges them in the oven. All the men work with the greatest exactness, and are, in truth like parts of the same machine. The business is to deposit in the oven seventy biscuits in a minute; and this is accomplished with the regularity of a clock, the clacking of the peel operating like the motion of the pendulum. There are twelve ovens at Deptford, and each will furnish daily bread for 2040 men.

It is said that scarcely any nation lives without bread or something as a substitute for it. In Lapland, where there is no corn, a kind of cake is made of dried fishes and the inner bark of the pine; this mixture would lead us to suppose that they did not expect nourishment from it, but only a dry substance which should be eaten, and would distend the stomach and bowels. The Norwegians make a bread that will keep thirty or forty years, and the inhabitants esteem old and stale bread far beyond that which is new so much so that particular care is taken to have the oldest bread at their great feasts. It frequently happens at the christening of a child that the guests are supplied with bread which has been baked at the birth of the father, or even grandfather. This bread is said to be made of barley and oats, and baked between two hollow stones.

STRAW-HAT-MAKER

There are few manufactures in the kingdom in which so little capital is wanted, or the knowledge of the art so soon acquired, as in that of straw-platting.

The straw-hat-maker is employed in the making up of hats only, after the straw is braided or platted.

The straw is cut at the joints; and the outer covering being removed, it is sorted of equal sizes, and made up into bundles of eight or ten inches in length, and a foot in circumference. These are then to be dipped in water, and shaken a little, so as not to retain too much moisture. and then the bundles are to be placed on their edges, in a box which is sufficiently close to prevent the evaporation of smoke. In the middle of the box is an earthen dish containing brim-stone broken in small pieces: this is set on fire, and the box covered over and kept in the open air several hours.

It will be the business of one person to split and select the straw for fifty others who are braiders. The splitting is done by a small machine made principally of wood. The straws, when split, are termed splints, of which each worker has a certain quantity: on one end is wrapped a linen cloth, and they are held under the arms and drawn out as wanted.

Platters should be taught to use their second fingers and thumbs, which are often required to assist in turning the splints, and facilitate very much the platting; they should also be cautioned against wetting the splint too much. Each platter should have a small linen work-bag; and a piece of pasteboard to roll the plat round. After five yards have been worked up, it should be wound about a piece of board half a yard wide, fastened at the top with yarn, and kept there several days to form it in a proper shape. Four of these parcels or a score is the measurement by which the plat is sold.

A good platter can make three score a week, and good work will always command a sale both in winter and in summer. The machines are small; they may be bought for two shillings each, and will last for many years.

When the straw is platted it comes into the hand of a person who sews it together into hats, bonnets, &c. of various sizes and shapes, according to the prevailing fashions. They are then put on wooden blocks for the purpose of hot-pressing; and to render them of a more delicate white, they are again exposed to the fumes of sulphur.

Persons who make up these hats will earn half-a-guinea a week: but braiders, or platters, if very expert, will earn much more.

THE SOAP BOILER

There is scarcely any substance manufactured by the art of man more useful than that of soap; at first sight it may seem strange, that the article which is used to clean and whiten other substances should itself be formed of grease or oil, and that the coarsest fat may be made into soap.

Soap is either hard or soft; it is variously named according to its colour: thus we have white, mottled, yellow soap, &c. But all kinds are made with fat or oil, combined with quick-lime and potash, or soda.

Quick lime is a substance well-known; *potash* is a salt obtained from vegetables in the following manner: — Vegetable substances, of any kind, burnt in the open air, and reduced to ashes, contain a certain proportion of salt, which is gained from the ashes by mixing them with water: and when the water is filtered, it is to be evaporated by heat, and the saline substance is left at the bottom of the vessel. This substance is called *potash*. *Soda* is obtained in the same way from the ashes of marine plants. Both potash and soda are called fixed *alkalis;* the *former* is denominated a *vegetable* alkali, the latter a *mineral* alkali.

The combination of soda, or potash, with oils or fat, forms soap: the union with *potash* affords *soft,* and the combination of *soda* with the same substances produces *hard,* soap.

The formation of *white* soap may be shown on a small scale, by the following simple process: Take by weight one part of lime, previously slaked, and two of soda; let them be boiled in twelve parts of water for half an hour, and then filter the fluid through a linen cloth till it is very clear. It must now be evaporated till a vial that would contain an ounce of water will hold an ounce and six drachms of the fluid. It is now called the *ley*. Mix one part of this ley with two parts of olive-oil in a glass or stone-ware vessel, and let it be beat up with a wooden spatula, and it soon becomes a consistent substance, and if left to stand four or five days it forms a white hard soap.

In large manufactories, the *ley* is made no stronger than to be able to sustain a new-laid egg; the workmen then begin to form the mixture. The oil or tallow is first boiled with a part of the *ley*, which may be diluted with water, till the whole is formed into soapy compound. The stronger *ley* is then to be added, and kept slowly boiling, while a person assists the union by constant agitation. When it is sufficiently boiled, a separation will appear to be taking place, the soap being at the top and the fluid below: to effect this separation completely, a quantity of common salt is added. The materials are usually boiled three or four hours; when the fire is withdrawn. The soap is found united at the top of the liquor, which is now called the *waste ley* , and being of no further use it is drawn off.

The soap is now melted for the last time with another ley, or with water and when a little boiled it is cast into wooden frames. These frames are moveable, and range exactly one upon another, and the soap is filled in from the bottom to the top. When it is perfectly set and cold, the workman takes off the upper frame, and with a piece of copper wire he cuts off the soap which that frame contained. He then takes off another frame, and so on till he comes to within five or six of the bottom, and there he finds the *ley* has drained from the soap into the middle of the substance; of course from this height to the bottom, the cakes of soap have an oval hole left in them. This ley he takes carefully out with an iron ladle, and puts into the bucket that stands before him. By the like process he cuts the soap into narrow slices, as it is usually sold in the shops.

In France they make a cheap soap by using woollen rags, old woollen cloths, and even the horn of animals, &c. instead of oil. These substances are all soluble in caustic ley, and by proper boiling form soap but it has a very disagreeable smell.

The tallow for making soap is reckoned very good if 13 cwt. of it, with alkali, will yield a ton weight of soap.

Yellow soap is made with tallow and resin, in the proportion of ten parts of tallow to three and a half of resin; and these, if good, will, with alkali, yield twenty of soap.

Mottled soap obtains its speckled appearance by dispersing the ley, towards the end of the operation, though the soap, or by adding to it a quantity of sulphate of iron, which, by its decomposition, deposits its oxide through the soap, and gives it the appearanace of streaked marble. Some manufacturers use the oxide of manganese for the same purpose.

Soap is easily and completely dissolved in soft water, but in hard water it curdles, or is only imperfectly dissolved: on this account a solution of soap in spirits of wine is used to discover whether water of any spring or pond be soft or hard; for if the water be soft the solution will unite with it, but it it be hard the soap will separate in flakes.

The soap manufacturer is subject to the excise laws, and he pays a heavy duty for every pound of soap that he makes. His coppers, and even furnace-doors, are furnished with locks and keys, and he dares not open them but in the presence of an excise-officer, and he must give notice of twenty-four hours or more, in writing to the officers before he begins making. His house is no longer an Englishman's castle, into which none may come but by his leave; the excise-officers are required to enter it at all times, by day and by night: who may, between the hours of five in the morning and eleven at night, unlock and examine every copper, and every part of the dwelling-house, none daring to obstruct them without incurring very heavy penalties. To similar restrictions the tallow-chandler, and other trades under the excise laws, are subject.

THE PLUMBER

The business of the plumber consists in the art of casting and working of lead and using it in buildings. He furnishes us with a cistern for water, and with a sink for the kitchen; he covers the house with lead, and makes the gutters to carry away the rain-water; he makes pipes of all sorts and sizes, and sometimes he casts leaden statues as ornaments for the garden. The plumber also is employed in making coffins for those who are to be interred out of the common way. And besides these departments in his trade, the modern plumber makes no small share of his profits by fitting up patent water-closets. Of these there are many different kinds, and but few inventions in modern days have answered so well to the patentees as these.

The chief articles in plumbery consisting in sheets and pipes of lead, we shall briefly describe the processes of making them.

In casting *sheet-lead* a sort of table, or mould, is used, about four or five feet wide, and sixteen or eighteen feet long; it must slope a little from the end in which the metal is poured on, and the slope must be greater in proportion to the thinness of the lead wanted. The mould is spread over with moistened sand about two inches thick, and made perfectly smooth by means of a piece of wood called a *strike*. At the upper end of the mould is a pan of a triangular shape. The lead, being melted, is put by means of ladles into this pan; and when it is cold enough, two men take the pan by the handle, (or else one of them lifts it by a bar and chain fixed to the beam in the ceiling,) and pour it into the mould, while another man stands ready with the *strike* to sweep the lead forwards, and draw the overplus into a trough ready to receive it. The sheets being thus cast, it remains only to roll them up or cut them to any particular size.

If a cistern is wanted, they measure out the four sides, and form any figures intended to be raised on the front in the sand, and cast as before; the sides are then soldered together after which, the bottom is soldered in.

Pipes are cast in a kind of mill, with arms or levers to turn it. The moulds are of hollow brass, consisting of two pieces, about two feet and a half long, which open and shut by means of hinges and hooks. In the middle of these moulds is placed a core or round solid piece of brass or iron, somewhat longer than the mould. This core is passed through two copper rundles, one at each end of the mould, which they serve to close; to these is joined a little copper tube two inches long, and of the thickness of the intended leaden pipe. These tubes retain the core exactly in the middle of the cavity of the mould, and then the lead is poured in through an aperture in the shape of a funnel. When the mould is full, a hook is put into the core, and turning the mill, it is drawn out, and the pipe is made. If it is to be lengthened, they put one end of it in the lower end of the mould, and the end of the core into it, then shut the mould again, and apply its rundle and tube as before, the pipe just cast serving for a rundle, &c. at the other end. Metal is again poured in which unites with the other pipe, and so the operation is repeated till the pipe is of the length required.

Large pipes of sheet-lead are made by wrapping the lead on wooden cylinders of the proper length, and then soldering it up the edges.

In this country it is not unfrequently that the business of glazier, plumber and painter, is united under the same person; but the plumbing trade is of itself, in London, reckoned a very good one for the master. The health of the men is often injured by the fumes of the lead. Journeymen earn about thirty shillings a week; and we recommend earnestly to lads brought up to either of the before mentioned trades, that they cultivate cleanliness and strict sobriety, and that they never on any account, eat their meals or retire to rest at night before they have well washed their hands and faces.

THE DYER

That the people of this country were not unacquainted with the the art of dyeing wool, yarn, and cloth of different colours, at a very early period, will need no proof here.

The art of dyeing the scarlet colour, however, by the help of a small insect of the kermes or cochineal kind, appears to have been discovered about A.D. 1000.

By an act of parliament passed in 1581 for abolishing certain deceitful stuff used in dyeing cloth, we find *logwood,* or blockwood, of late years brought into this "realm," expressly prohibited; "the colour thereof being false and deceitful to the Queen's subjects at home, and discreditable beyond sea to our merchants and dyers." Its use was again prohibited in 1497, as well as in the reign of James. But in 1661 the different laws prohibiting its use were repealed, it being found that "the ingenious industry of these times hath taught the dyers of England the art of fixing the colours made of logwood, *alias* blackwood, so as that by experience they are found as lasting and serviceable as the colours made with any other sort of dyeing wood."

The art of the dyer consists in tingeing cloth, stuff, or other substances with a permanent colour which penetrates its substance. Dyeing differs from bleaching, which is not the giving a new colour but brightening an old one. It differs also from painting, printing, or stamping because the colours in these only reach the surface.

The mystery of the art of dyeing consists chiefly in chemical processes, and it comprises a vast collection of chemical ex periments. The substances principally subjected to this art are wool, hair, silk, cotton, hemp, and flax. Of these the animal productions, namely, wool, hair, and silk, take the dye more readily than the vegetable substances, cotton, hemp, and flax, because they seem to have a stronger attraction for the colouring particles of the various dyes employed.

Wool is naturally of a greasy nature, and requires to be scoured before it is submitted to the process of dyeing.

Silk, previously to dyeing, must be washed with soap and warm water, and then in a cold solution of alum and water.

Cottons and *linens* require bleaching, and scouring in alkaline ley. After this they must be steeped in a strong solution of alum and water then washed in clear water and afterwards rensed in a decoction of galls or some other astringent, as hot as the workman can bear it.

The first step in dyeing is the application of what is termed a *mordant;* that is, something must be employed to make the substances take the dye; for by merely immersing them into the dyeing liquor they will seldom take or retain a deep dye.

Different mordants are used for preparing different goods, and for preparing the same goods for different colouring drugs. Alum is the most extensively useful, being always employed in the case of linens and cottons. For the dyeing of silk and wool, metallic solutions are more frequently employed as mordants, because these have a stronger attraction for animal than vegetable substances.

In dyeing, there are but three simple colours, the *red, yellow,* and *blue;* all other colours are compounded of these. Different shades or tints of the same colour are produced by using different drugs, or by varying the quantity of colouring particles.

Cochineal, kermes, and gum-lac, among the animal productions, and madder, archil, carthamus, and Brazil wood, among the vegetables, are the chief substances employed as *red* dyes.

All the substances employed for dyeing *yellow* colours are vegetable productions; and the principal *blue* dyes are from indigo, woad, logwood, and Prussian blue.

Compound colours are produced sometimes by mixing the simple colours in the dyeing liquor, and sometimes by dyeing the stuff first in a bath of one simple colour then in another.

In London there are dyers of all sorts; some dye only wool, others silk; some confine themselves to particular colours, such as scarlet and blues. The scarlet dyeing is said to be the most ingenious and most profitable. The business of a dyer of woollens is laborious and chilly, the workmen are constantly dabbling in water hot and cold. Silk dyers have the least laborious business; journeymen will easily earn thirty shillings a week.

THE POTTER

Pottery, or the art of making vessels of baked earth, is of very remote antiquity. The antient Greeks and Etruscans particularly excelled in it. Porcelain, the most perfect species of pottery, has been made in China from time immemorial.

Clay and flints are substances of which every kind of earthen-ware is made: clay alone shrinks and cracks, the flint gives it solidity and strength.

The wheel and the lathe are the chief instruments in the business of pottery: the first is intended for large works, and the other for small: the wheel is turned by a labourer, but the lathe is put into motion by the foot of the workman.

When the clay is properly prepared, and made into lumps proportioned to the size of the cup, plate, or other vessel to be made, the potter places one of these lumps upon the head of the wheel before him, which he turns round, while he forms the cavity of the vessel with his finger and thumb, continuing to widen it from the middle, and thus turning the inside into form with one hand, while he proportions the outside with the other, the wheel being kept the whole time in constant motion. The mouldings are formed by holding a piece of wood or iron, cut into the shape of the moulding, to the vessel while the wheel is going round; but the feet and handles are made by themselves, and set on by the hand; and if there be any sculpture in the work, it is usually made in wooden moulds, and stuck on piece by piece on the outside of the vessel. When the vessel is finished, the workman cuts it off from the remaining part of the clay, and sets it aside to dry; and when it is hardened sufficiently to bear removing without danger, it is covered with a glazing made of a composition of lead, and put into a furnace, where it is baked. Some sorts are glazed by throwing sea-salt into the furnace, among the different pieces of pottery. The salt is decomposed, and its vapours form a glazing upon the vessel: which is not however much esteemed, it was introduced into England by two brothers from Holland of the names of Elers about the year 1700, who settled in the neighbourhood of the Staffordshire potteries.

English stone-ware is made of tobacco-pipe clay, mixed with flints calcined and ground. This mixture burns white, and vessels of this kind were formerly all glazed with sea-salt. Wedgewood's *queen's ware* is made of tobbaco-pipe clay, much beaten in water. By this process the finer parts of the clay remain suspended in the water, while the coarser and all impurities fall to the bottom. The thick liquid is further purified by passing it through hair and lawn sieves, after which it is mixed with another liquid consisting of flints calcined, ground and suspended in water. The mixture is then dried in a kiln; and being afterwards beaten to a proper temper, it becomes fit for being formed at the wheel into dishes, plates, bowls, &c.

When this ware is to be put into the furnace to be baked, the several pieces of it are placed in cases made of clay, which are piled one upon another in the dome of the furnace; a fire is then lighted, and the ware is brought into a proper temper for glazing. By being baked the ware acquires a strong property of imbibing moisture; in this state it is called *biscuit;* and when dipped into the glaze, consisting of water made thick with white lead and ground flints, it attracts it into its pores, and the ware presently becomes dry. It is then exposed a second time to the fire, and the lead forms a glossy coat on the surface which is more or less yellow, according as a greater or less proportion of that metal has been used. The use of ground flints in the potteries was introduced in the following manner: about the year 1720, a potter travelling to London on horseback had occasion at Dunstable to seek a remedy for a disorder in his horses's eyes: the ostler of the inn, by burning a flint stone reduced it to a fine powder which he blew into them. The potter observing the beautiful white colour of the flint after calcination instantly conceived the uses to which it might be applied in his art and then introducing the white pipe clay found in the north of Devonshire instead of the drossy clays of his own country, readily produced the white stone ware, the flint serves only to give a consistency to the lead during the time of its vitrification.

45

THE TYPE-FOUNDER

The first part of the type-founder's business is to prepare the metal, which is a composition of lead and regulus of antimony, melted together in a furnace. In large founderies this metal is cast into bars of twenty pounds each, which are delivered to the workmen as occasion may require; this is a laborious and unwholesome part of the business, owing to the fumes which are thrown off. Fifteen hundred weight of this metal is cast in a day, and the founders usually cast as much at one casting as will last six months.

We now come to the letter cutter; that is, to him who cuts the moulds in which the letters are cast; he must be provided with vices, hammers, files, gravers, and gauges of various kinds. He then prepares steel punches, on the face of which he draws or marks the exact shape of the letter, and with pointed gravers and sculpters he digs out the steel between the strokes or marks which he made on the face of the punch, leaving the marks standing. Having shaped the inside strokes of the letter, he deepens the hollows with the same tools: for if a letter be not deep in proportion to its width, it will when used at press, print black, and be good for nothing. He then works the outside with files till it is fit for the matrice.

A matrice is a piece of brass or copper about an inch and half long, and thick in proportion to the size of the letter it is to contain. In this metal is sunk the face of the letter intended to be cast, by striking the letter-punch. After this the sides and face of the matrice must be cleared, with files, of all bunchings made by sinking the punch.

When the metal and other things are properly prepared, the matrice is fastened to the end of the mould, which the caster holds in his left hand, while he pours the metal in with his right; by a sudden jerk of the hand the metal runs into the cavity of matrice and takes the figure or impression. The mould consists of an under and an upper half, of which the latter is taken off as soon as the letter is cast, he then throws the letter upon a sheet of paper, laid for the purpose on a bench or table, and he is ready to cast another letter as before.

When the casters have made a certain number of types, which are made much longer than they are wanted, boys come and break away the jets or extra lengths from the types; the jets they cast into the pot, and the types are carried to the man who polishes their broad sides. This is a very dexterous operation; for the man, in turning up the types, does it so quickly, by a mere touch of the fingers of the left hand, as not to require the least perceptible intermission in the motion of the right hand upon the stone.

The caster pours the metal into the mould. He takes it up with a small ladle from the pan, which is constantly kept over the fire in a sort of stove under the brick-work. The iron plate defends him from the heat of the fire, and a screen between the two workmen is to prevent the other man from being injured by the metal, which is apt to fly about by the operation of casting. Near the newly cast types are several blocks of the metal, with which the caster replenishes his pan as he makes the letters.

A type-founder will cast upwards of 3000 letters in a day; and the perfection of letters thus cast, consists in their being all straight and square; of the same height, and evenly lined, without sloping one way or the other.

What is called a fount or font of letter, is a quantity of each kind cast by the letter-founder and properly sorted. A complete font includes, besides the running letters, all the single letters, double letters, points, commas, lines, borders, head and tail pieces and numerical characters.

Letter-founders have a kind of list by which they regulate their founts; this is absolutely necessary, as some letters are much more frequently used than others, of course the cells containing these should be better stored than those of the letters which do not so often recur. Thus a fount does not contain an equal number of *a* and *b,* or of *c* and *z.* In a fount containing a hundred thousand characters, the *a* should have five thousand, the *c* three thousand, the *e* eleven thousand, the i six thousand, and the other letters in proportion.

Printers order their founts either by the hundred weight or by the sheet. If they order a fount of five hundred they mean that the whole shall weigh about 500lb. but if they require a fount of ten sheets, it is understood, that with this fount they shall be able to compose ten sheets, or twenty forms, without being obliged to distribute. The founder reckons 120 lb. to a sheet, but this varies with the nature of the letter.

THE COACH-MAKER

The coach-maker makes coaches, chaises of all kinds, and other vehicles for travelling. These kinds of carriages were not known in Europe till the beginning of the sixteenth century, when they were used only by women of the first rank, it being considered disgraceful for men to ride in them. At that period, in Germany, when the electors and princes did not wish to be present at the meetings of the states, they excused themselves by informing the emperor, that their health would not permit them to ride on horseback.

The oldest carriages used by the ladies in England were known under the now forgotten name of *whirlicotes.*

According to Stow, coaches were introduced here from Germany by the earl of Arundel, about the year 1580, but it was not till more than twenty years after this that they began to be used generally. The celebrated duke of Buckingham was the person who rode in a coach with six horses. To ridicule this new pomp, the earl of Northumberland put eight horses to his carriage.

Coaches consist of two principal parts, the *body* and the *carriage.* The body is that part which is intended for the passengers; the carriage is that which sustains the body, and to which the wheels, that give motion to the whole machine are fastened.

The business of a coach-maker is divided into several parts, as will be seen at the conclusion of this article.

The body of the coach is built chiefly with ash, but the pannels are generally made of mahogany; the upper parts are covered with well dressed and highly varnished leather. The inside of a coach is lined with woollen cloths, and stuffed with horse hair. Coaches, however, made in very high style, are lined with silk, sometimes with velvet, and not unfrequently with exceedingly fine and beautiful leather.

The carriage consists principally of two pair of wheels, with axle-trees, and a perch.

The perch is that long pole which is fastened to the middle of the hind axle-tree, and passes between the fore axle and its bolster, being secured by the pole-pin, so as to move about it, and connecting the fore and hind wheels together. It is plain, that in turning a carriage of this construction, the larger the wheel the sooner it will strike against the perch: on account of the axle being under the perch, and to accommodate some other contrivance in the lower part of the carriage, the fore-wheels are usually made smaller than the hind ones.

Coaches are distinguished with regard to the structure, into coaches, chariots, landaus, berlins, &c. some of which, as the two last, take their names from the places at which they were first made.

Coaches are also distinguished according to the uses for which they are designed: thus we have travelling coaches, stage-coaches, hackney-coaches, &c.

Chaises also, the making of which forms a considerable part of a coach-maker's business, have different names, and have very different constructions: thus we have post-chaises, gigs, curricles, tandems, &c. The first is a sort of chariot without a box.

Hackney-coaches are those which are stationed at certain stands in the streets of London, and other large cities for the convenience of passengers, and are hired at rates fixed by authority. These were introduced into London about the year 1625, when they were only twenty: in 1715 the number was limited to 800; and now there are 1100 which ply in the streets of London every day, Sundays excepted, on which day the number is much less. Hackney-coachmen are subject to strict regulations, and liable to be punished for any offences, or for over charges. Coaches on the most elegant construction are made in London, whence they are exported to the continent, the East Indies and America; indeed they are made more elegant for the East Indies than those retained in this country.

Modern European coaches were unknown in China till Lord Macartney's embassy to that empire. With his lordship, two of Hatchet's most splendid carriages were sent as presents to the emperor. These puzzled the Chinese more than any of the other presents. Nothing of the kind had ever been seen at that capital; and the disputes among themselves, as to the part which was intended for the seat of the emperor, were whimsical enough. The hammer-cloth that covered the box of the winter carriage had a smart edging, and was ornamented with festoons of roses. Its splendid appearance and elevated situation determined it at once, in the opinion of the majority, to be the emperor's seat; but a difficulty arose how to appropriate the inside of the carriage. They examined the windows, the blinds, and the screens; and as last concluded, that it could be for nobody but his ladies. An old eunuch sought particularly for information: and when he learned that the fine elevated box was to be the seat of the man who managed the horses, and that the emperor's place was within, he asked with a sneer, if it could be supposed that the emperor would suffer any man to sit higher than himself, and to turn his back towards him? He wished the coach-box to be removed, and placed behind the body of the carriage.

The business of a coach-maker is divided into several branches, whose wages are in proportion to the nicety of their work, thus;—the body-makers in general, having two to three pounds per week — the carriage-makers between one and two pounds — the trimmers about two guineas — the painters from twenty to thirty shillings — the body painters about forty shillings — the herald painters, from three to four pounds — smiths about thirty shillings.

49

THE TALLOW CHANDLER.

In France, and in other countries on the continent, the person who exercises the profession of tallow-chandler is called by the more appropriate name of candle-maker.

A candle is a cotton wick loosely twisted and covered with tallow wax, or spermaceti, in a cylindrical figure; which being lighted at the end, serves to illuminate the place in the absence of the sun.

Tallow candles should be made of equal parts of bullocks' and sheep's tallow. They are of two kinds; the one dipped, the other moulded.

The cotton used for dipped or common candles is brought from Smyrna in the wool, which grows on trees like nuts enclosed in a shell, and is here carded and spun into balls. The cotton for mould comes from Turkey and the adjacent places, packed in bales, which before being landed in England is made to perform quarantine.

The tallow-chandler employs women to wind the cotton into large balls: he then takes five, six, or eight balls, and, drawing out the threads from each, cuts them into proper lengths according to the size of the candles wanted.

The machine for cutting the cotton is a piece of smooth board made to be fixed on the knees: on the upper surface is the blade of a razor, and a round piece of cane, placed at a certain distance from one another, according to the length of the cotton wanted: the cotton is carried round the cane, and, being brought to the razor, is instantly separated from the several balls.

The next operation is what is denominated *pulling the cotton,* by which the threads are laid smooth, and knots and unevennesses removed, and in short, the cotton is rendered fit for use. It is now spread, that is, for dipped candles placed at equal distances, over rods about half an inch in diameter, these are called broaches; they are something more than three feet long.

The Tallow-chandlers' business in London is generally performed in a cellar.

The tallow is first melted in a large copper, and after it is well skimmed and refined it is brought into a vessel called a *mould,* in which the cottons are dipped. The workman holds three of these broaches between his fingers, and immerses the cottons into the mould: they are then hung on a frame for the purpose, till they become cold and hard; during which others are dipped. When cold, they are dipped a second and a third time, and so on till the candles are of the proper size.

During the operation, the tallow is stirred frequently, and the mould supplied with fresh tallow, which is kept to the proper heat by means of a fire under it.

Such was the laborious method universally adopted in making common candles, till within these fifteen or twenty years, when an invention was introduced. Three pulleys are let into a beam of the house; round these proper-sized ropes run, and are fixed to a machine on which six broaches are placed. In the scale are weights sufficient to draw up the broaches; these are increased as the candles become larger and heavier. The workman, by means of this very simple and excellent contrivance, has only to guide the candles, and not to support the weight of them between his fingers. The frames in which the moulded candles are cast is of wood, and the several moulds are hollow metal cylinders, generally made of pewter, of the diameter and length of the candle wanted: at the extremity of these is the neck, which is a little cavity, in form of a dome, having a moulding within side, and pierced in the middle, with a hole big enough for the cotton to pass through. The cotton is introduced into the shaft of the mould, by a piece of wire being thrust through the aperture of the hook till it comes out of the neck: the other end of the cotton is so fastened as to keep it in a perpendicular situation, and in the middle of the candle; the moulds are then filled with warm tallow, and left to be very cold before they can be drawn out of the pipes.

Besides these, there are other candles made by tallow-chandlers intended to burn during the night, without the necessity of snuffing; the wick has been usually made of split rushes; but lately very small cotton wicks have been substituted for the rush; these are lighted much easier, are less liable to got out, and, owing to the smallness of the cotton, do not require the aid of snuffers.

The business of most tallow-chandlers includes the melting of tallow, which is done by chopping the fat as it is taken from oxen and sheep, and then boiling it for some time in a large copper, and when the tallow is sufficiently melted and the fluid part draws off, the remainder is subjected to the operation of a strong iron press, and the cake that is left after the tallow is by this means completely expressed is called a greave: with this dogs are fed, as well as the greater part of the ducks that are reared in the vale of Aylesbury, from whence the London markets in a great degree are supplied; it is also sometimes given to oxen and pigs, but certainly without benefiting the flavour of the meat.

Large quantities of tallow are every year imported from Russia in casks; from which are manufactured soap and inferior candles.

The price of candles in London used formerly to be regulated by the master and wardens of the tallow-chandlers' company, who met at their hall on Dowgate Hill every month for the purpose. But now the price of every article belonging to the trade is fixed at the weekly markets.

Journeymen generally board in their master's house, and receive from twenty to thirty pounds a year exclusive of boards. There are also daymen, who work by the day, and are paid according to the number of candles made. Besides their common wages, it is the custom of the trade to allow *beer-money*.

THE GARDENER

A gardener is employed in the management and cultivation of fruit-trees, flowers, plants, and vegetables of all kinds.

Gardens are distinguished into *flower, fruit,* and *kitchen-gardens*. The first are for pleasure and ornament and are, therefore, placed in the most conspicuous situation; the two latter are for service, and made in more obscure and retired places. They were formerly distinct, but they are now generally united, because they both require a good soil and exposure, and are generally placed out of view of the house.

The principal operations of the gardener are planting and transplanting, engrafting, inoculating, pruning, sowing, &c. Most of these are so well understood, that we shall only speak on the subject of *engrafting*, which is the art of inserting a shoot of one tree in the stock of another, in order to correct or improve its fruit.

The implements necessary for this business are a grafting-knife, a quantity of strong bass strings for bandages, to tie the stocks and grafts firmly together, and some well wrought clay to put over the tying, to secure them from the air and the wet.

When the grafts or shoots, which must be of the last year's growth, are quite ready, fix upon a smooth par of the stock, and then pare off the rind with a little of the wood in a sloping direction about an inch in length; then, having the shoots cut into lengths with four or five eyes on each, prepare one to fit the stock exactly, then cut a slit or tongue about half an inch in length upwards in the shoot, and another the same length downwards in the stock to receive it, and in that manner fix the graft in the stock, taking care that the sap and rind of both may join as exactly as possible in every part. Having thus fixed the graft, let it be immediately tied with a string of soft bass, bringing it several times round the graft and stock, taking care to preserve the graft in its due position; and let the bandage be neatly tied, and the place be covered with some grafting clay, in such a manner that neither the air, the rays of the sun, nor the wet, can enter. This is called whip-grafting, and is only one of several ways in which engrafting is performed by Europeans.

The Chinese, in place of raising trees from seeds or from grafts, as is the custom in Europe, have adopted the following method of increasing them.

They select a tree of that species which they wish to propagate, and fix upon such a branch as will least hurt or disfigure the tree by its removal.

Round this branch and as near as they can conveniently to its junction with the trunk, they wind a rope, made of straw, besmeared with cow-dung, until a ball is formed, five or six times the diameter of the branch. This is intended as a bed into which the young roots may shoot. Having performed this part of the operation, they immediately under the ball divide the bark down to the wood, for nearly two-thirds of the circumference of the branch. A cocoa-nut shell or small pot is then hung over the ball, with a hole in its bottom, so small that water put therein will only fall in drops, by this the rope is constantly kept moist, a circumstance necessary to the easy admission of the young roots, and to the supply of nourishment to the branch from this new channel.

During three succeeding weeks, nothing further is required, except supplying the vessels with water. At the expiration of that period one-third of the remaining bark is cut, and the former incision is carried considerably deeper into the wood, as by this time it is expected that some roots have struck into the rope, and are giving their assistance in support of the branch.

After a similar period the same operation is repeated, and in about two months from the commencement of the process, the roots may generally be seen intersecting each other on the surface of the ball, which is a sign that they are sufficiently advanced to admit of the separation of the branch from the tree. This is best done by sawing it off at the incision, care being taken that the rope, which by this time is nearly rotten, is not shaken off by the motion. The branch is then planted as a young tree.

It appears probably, that to succeed with this operation in Europe, a longer period would be necessary, vegetation being much slower in Europe than in India, the chief field of my experiments. I am, however, of opinion, from some trials which I have lately made on cherry trees, that an additional month would be adequate to make up for the deficiency of climate.

The advantage to be derived from this method are, that a further growth of three or four years is sufficient, when the branches are of any considerable size, to bring them to their full bearing state, whereas, even in India, eight or ten years are necessary with most kinds of fruit trees, if raised from the seed.

There are several kinds of gardeners; some gain a living by looking after other people's gardens; for which they receive a certain sum per annum, according to the size of the garden. Others live in gentlemen's houses, and, like domestics in general, receive wages for their labour, from twenty to a hundred pounds per annum, according to their merit, or to what may be expected from them. Some gardeners go out to day-work, whose wages are from three to five shillings a day.

Besides these we have market-gardeners, that is, persons who raise vegetables and fruit, which they expose to sale in markets and other places. Gardens, for the raising of vegetables for sale, were first cultivated about Sandwich in Kent. The example was soon followed near the metropolis; and perhaps there is not a finer sight any where than Covent-Garden market, about six or seven o'clock in the morning of a Saturday, during the early part of the summer.

Within a few miles of the metropolis, there are supposed to be about five thousand acres of land constantly cultivated for the supply of the London markets with garden vegetables, exclusive of about eight hundred acres cropped with fruit of various kinds and about seventeen hundred acres cultivated for potatoes.

In the parish of Fulham, the cultivation of gardens for the market, is carried on to a greater extent than in any other part in the kingdom. The parishes of St. Paul's, Deptford, Chiswick, Battersea, and Mortlake, are celebrated for their asparagus. Deptford is also famous for the culture of onions for seed of which, on an aveage, there are about twenty acres annually.

THE HAIR-DRESSER

The hair-dresser cuts and dresses ladies' and gentlemen's hair; he makes wigs and braids, and in most cases the business includes the art of shaving

The hair-dresser requires scissors, combs, some powder and pomatum, things too well known to stand in need of description. The business was in much greater repute ten years ago than it is at present. In the year 1795 an annual tax of one guinea was laid upon all persons who should in future wear hair-powder so this very much injured the trade: the following year, and also the year 1799, were seasons of uncommon scarcity with regard to wheat, from which hair-powder is manufactured; this circumstance led many others to abandon the fashion of hair-dressing.

The principal requisites in a hair-dresser are, a light hand, an aptness in catching the changing fashions of the times, and a taste to improve upon them.

Perukes or wigs are also less in fashion among gentlemen than they were formerly; but perhaps they were never more common among the fair sex than at present; and if we may judge from the splendid appearance of many shops in which ladies' wigs, braids, and curls are manufactured, no business is more flourishing or more profitable.

The fashion of wearing wigs and false hair is not peculiar to modern times; it was common to the Greeks and Romans. The peruke of the emperor Commodus is described as having been powdered with scrapings of gold, which were made to adhere to the hair by means of glutinous perfumes.

Perukes in their present form were introduced into Paris in the year 1629, whence they have spread, by degrees, though the rest of Europe. At first it was reputed a scandal for young people to wear wigs, because the loss of their hair at that age was attributed to a disease which was in itself disgraceful. They are now become so common, that few ladies, notwithstanding they possess the most beautiful hair, would be thought to be without false hair: and some, supposing that they can improve on nature, change their own for hair of a very different colour. Hence we sometimes see a fair skin and light eyes decorated with black hair; and a dark complexion with black sparkling eyes set off with flaxen locks! Such is the taste at the commencement of the nineteenth century.

Hair makes a very considerable article in commerce. The merit of good hair consists in it being well fed, and neither too coarse nor too slender; the largeness rendering it less susceptible of the artificial curl, and the smallness making its curl of too short duration.

There is no certain price for hair but it is sold from five shillings to five pounds per ounce, according to its quality and colour.

Hair which does not curl naturally is brought to it by boiling, and by baking in the following manner: after having sorted the hair, it is rolled and afterwards fastened upon little cylindrical instruments, either of wooden or earthen ware, called pipes, in which state it is put into a vessel over the fire, and boiled about two hours; it is then taken out and dried and sent to be baked in the oven.

Hair thus prepared is woven on strong thread, which is sewed on a cawl, fitted to the head for a peruke.

Formerly peruke-makers made no difference between the ends of the hair, but curled and wove them by either indifferently; but it is now known that hair to curl well must be woven by the end which grows next the head.

Perukes much worn may with attention be made to look very smart, so long as they are kept from the wet; a circumstance which reminds one of an amusing anecdote.

"One day says an avaricious doctor in Lancashire to his barber's lad, Jack, can't you take this old wig of mine and dress it up a bit? I'll give you a shilling: but be sure you don't let your master know." The lad closed with the offer, but, feeling no fondness for his employer, told his master and fellow-apprentices of his private job; to work he went with irons so hot as scorched and destroyed the hair eventually, but kept for a time a fresh and stiff curl to the eye. 'Aye! this is well done, Jack, indeed:—there's a shilling for you.' In a day or two the doctor went out in this *renovated busby;* but meeting unfortunately with a heavy shower in his ride, the curls hung down never to be raised again, and betrayed the canker at the root!

"When Jack made his regular visit the next day, he saw the doctor ready equipped with a horse whip in his hand to give him a warm reception. Jack's conscience smote him, he took to his heels, and consigned the beard and periwig of his reverence to another artist."

The operation of shaving, which is another part of a hair-dresser's business, stands in need of no description; the great art depends on a light hand and a good razor.

Mr. Nicholson in an early volume of his Chemical Journal has favoured us with a scientific account of this business, which we refer to with peculiar pleasure, as it shews that nothing ought to be beneath the attention of a man of science.

Journeymen hair-dressers earn from fifteen shillings to a guinea per week; but those who work on wig-making, and the wearing of hair, will, if very expert, earn much more than this.

THE COMB-MAKER

The use of combs is too well known to stand in need of any description. They are generally made of the horn of bullocks, or of elephants and sea horse's teeth: some are made of tortoise-shell, and others of box or holly woods. Bullocks' horns are thus prepared in order to manufacture combs: the tips are first sawn off, they are then held in the flame of the wood fire; this is called roasting, by which they become nearly as soft as leather. While in that state they are split open on one side and pressed in a machine between two iron plates, they are then plunged into a trough of water, from which they come out hard and flat.

After the horn is cut to the intended size, three or four pieces are laid upon a pair of tongs over a fire of joiner's shavings to soften them; they are turned as many times, and when sufficiently soft are put into a vice and screwed tight to complete the flattening; they are suffered to remain a while until they become perfectly flat and hard again; they are then given to a man who shaves, planes, or scrapes off the rough parts by a knife with two handles (similar to those used by the coopers) which he works from him across the grain of the horn, from one end of the intended comb to the other; when both sides are perfectly smooth, it is delivered to the person who cuts the teeth; he fastens it by that part meant for the back, into an instrument for holding it, called a "clam," by wedges; the clam has a long handle, which the workman places under him as he sits; by this means he steadies the object of his work, as both his hands are to be employed in the operation. The cutting of the teeth is commenced by a double saw, each blade of which is like the small one with which joiners and cabinet-makers cut their fine work; with this he forms the teeth, but as this instrument leaves the work square and rough in the inside edge of each tooth, it is followed by another about the size and shape of a case knife, having teeth like a file, on each flat side; after this two others of the same shape, but each finer cut than the other follow, one stroke on each side of the comb is then given by a rasping tool (in which also a little attention is used to give the ends of the teeth a small bevel or angle); this tool is used to take off any roughness that may remain on the sides of the teeth; it is now delivered to another operator, who polishes it with rotten stone and oil, applying them with a piece of buff leather; after which the article is ready for sale.

The process used for making ivory combs is nearly the same as that already described, except that the ivory is first sawed into thin slices. The best ivory comes from the island of Ceylon and Achen, in the East Indies, this has the property of never turning yellow; of course the ivory from these places is much dearer than that brought from other parts.

Having described the usual method of making combs, it is right to inform the reader, that about eight years ago Mr. Bundy, of Camden Town, obtained a patent for cutting combs by means of machinery. It will be thought a very singular circumstance, that, before this period, no method was practised in this country for cutting the teeth of combs, but that in which a pair of saws, rudely fastened in a wooden back, was directed by the human hand. With these implements, however, it is, that the very delicate superfine ivory combs, containing from fifty to sixty teeth in an inch, are manufactured.

By Mr. Bundy's machine the business of comb-making is greatly expedited; the teeth of two combs may be cut in about three minutes. The combs are afterwards pointed by applying them to an arbor or axis clothed with cutters having chamfered edges and teeth.

Tortoise-shell combs are very much used, and there are methods of staining horn so as to imitate tortoise-shell; of which the following is one:— The horn to be dyed must be first pressed into a flat form, and then spread over with a paste made of two parts of quick-lime and one of litharge, brought into a proper consistence with soap-ley. This paste must be put over all the parts of the horn, except such as are proper to be left transparent, to give it a nearer resemblance to tortoise-shell. The horn must remain in this state till the paste be quite dry, when it is to be brushed off. It requires taste and judgement to dispose the paste in such a manner as to form a variety of transparent parts, of different magnitudes and figures, to look like nature. Some parts should also be semi-transparent; which may be effected by mixing whiting with a part of the paste to weaken its operation in particular places; by this means spots of a reddish brown will be produced so as greatly to increase the beauty of the work. Horn thus dyed is manufactured into combs, and these are frequently sold for real tortoise-shell.

Combs are not only made for the purpose of cleaning the hair, but for ornament; they are sometimes set with brilliant stones, pearls, and even diamonds; some again are studded with cut steel; these are of different shapes, and are used to fasten up the hair when ladies dress without caps. Of course combs may be had of all prices, from the value of a few pence to almost any sum. Journeymen comb-makers will earn a guinea or thirty shillings a week.

Horn, from which combs are generally made, when very thin becomes transparent, and has been used instead of glass for windows. When heated it may be bent to any shape, and wrought into trinkets of all forms. Tortoise-shell, upon being analyzed, is found to consist of very thin membranes laid over each other, and is in its nature very like the nails that defend the human toes and fingers from injury.

THE LACE-MAKER

The Lace-maker is often engaged in her work in the open air — even in this country no uncommon sight during the summer months.

Lace is not woven, and of course it requires in the operation neither warp nor woof. It is made of silk or of thread, which is wound on little bobbins, made of bone or ivory, about the thickness of a skewer: hence the name bone-lace. The pattern, to which the lace is to be made, is drawn on paper or parchment, pricked with pin-holes, and then put on the pad or cushion which the woman holds on her knees. All the ends of the thread are first fastened together, and the lace-maker twists them variously, over and under each other, round the pins, which are stuck into the holes of the pattern: these pins they remove from one part to another, as their work goes on; and by these means are produced that multiplicity of eyes, or openings, which give to lace the desired figures.

For this operation much art and ingenuity are not necessary: it is however, very tedious work; and when the thread is fine, and the pattern full and complex, it requires a degree of attention which can rarely be expected in persons of easy circumstances. Lace-making, therefore, is consigned to the hands of indigent women and young girls, who by their skill and dexterity, raise the value of material, originally of little worth, to almost any sum. But the hammer. Anvils are sometimes made of cast iron; but the best are those which are forged, with the upper part made of steel. The whole is usually mounted on a firm wooden block.

the time required to accomplish this beautiful manufacture is always in proportion to value of the work; so that after all, little money is earned in the business.

The origins of the art of lace-making cannot be distinctly traced; by some it has been supped to be the same as that which is called in Latin authors the *Phrygian art*; but this probably consisted rather in needle-work, than in that sort of netting used in the making of bone-lace. Borders sewed upon cloths and tapestry, which are mentioned by ancient writers, were a kind of lace worked with a needle: this lace is undoubtedly of much older date than that made by netting. Of the former kind much is still extant among old church-furniture, which was probably the work of nuns, or ladies of fortune, who devoted their time to the business on religious motives! But if it had been manufactured as an article of commerce, something more would have been found concerning it in contemporary authors.

A lace manufactory was established in Paris, under the auspices of the celebrated Colbert, in the year 1666 but this was done by the needle, and was similar to what is called *point*.

The Germans, however, claim the honour of having invented the art of lace-making by means of the cushion and bobbins: they ascribe the invention to Barbara, the wife of Christopher Uttmann, who died about the year 1575. At this period the mines in Germany were become much less productive than they had been for centuries; the wives and daughters therefore, of the miners, were induced to turn their hands to the making of lace, which owing to the low price of labour, they were enabled to sell so cheap, that it became fashionable, in opposition to the Italian lace worked with the needle, and even supplanted it in commerce.

The best laces are now made at Mechlin, Brussels, Ghent, Antwerp, and Valenciennes, which still enrich the country around, and induce the farmers to cultivate flax on the poorest soils. In France, lace was made in large quantities in the convents.

In our own country, the manufacture of lace is carried on to a greater extent and perfection in Buckinghamshire than in any other part of the United Kingdom, particularly in the town and neighbourhood of Newport-Pagnel, which is a sort of mart for that article, and flourishes considerably by its means.

THE MILLINER

The business of the milliner, and the articles which she makes up for sale, include hats, caps, bonnets, cloaks, muffs and fur tippets. Articles belonging to her trade include feathers, artificial flowers, muslin, gauze, crape, ribbons of different widths, colours and prices, thread, laces etc.

In the milliner taste and fancy are required, with a quickness in discerning, imitating, and improving upon the various fashions, which are perpetually changing among the higher circles.*

Silks and satins of various sorts are much used in this business, which formerly, were chiefly imported into this country, but are now manufactured in great perfection in Spital and its neighbourhood.

Gauze is a very thin, slight, transparent kind of stuff, woven sometimes of silk, and sometimes only of thread. The gauze-loom does not differ very much from the common weaver's loom, but it has some peculiar appendages. There are a great variety of gauzes; some with flowers on a silk ground, some wrought with gold and silver. Gauze is chiefly made in this country, but part of what is used here is brought from China.

Crape is a very light transparent stuff, in some respects like gauze: but it is made of raw silk, gummed and twisted on the mill, and woven without crossing. It is used for mourning, and is now a very fashionable article in court dresses. Crapes used for mourning are either *crisped* or *smooth:* the first is *double,* and denotes the deeper mourning; the *single* or smooth crape is for the slighter. Crapes are of different colours, but the silk is always dyed in its raw state. The chief manufacture for this article of dress, is at Lyons, but a great deal is made in various parts of this kingdom.

Crapes, when made into court dresses are ornamented in a thousand different ways: sometimes as caps, or turbans, they are ornamented with *spangles, artificial flowers,* and *diamonds.*

Spangles are small thin round leaves of metal pierced in the middle, which are sewed on as ornaments to a dress. They are made in the following manner: a wire is twisted in the form of a screw; it is then cut into single spiral rings, like those used by pin-makers; and these rings, being placed on a very smooth anvil, are flatted, and spread by a smart blow of the hammer, so that a small hole remains in the middle; and the ends of the wire which lie over each other are closely united. Spangles were first made in the gold and silver manufactories of France, and this method was long kept a secret: at length, however, they were successfully imitated in Germany and other parts.

Artificial flowers are made, sometimes of very fine coloured paper, sometimes of the inside linings upon which the silk-worm spins its silk, but principally of cambric, which is a kind of linen made of flax, first manufactured at Cambray, in France, of which great quantities were imported into this country: but now persons convicted of wearing, or selling, or making up for hire, any cambric of French lawns are liable to a penalty of 5l. The cambrics chiefly in use here are manufactured in Scotland and Ireland.

Ribbons used by the milliners are woven: of these there are several sorts distinguished by different names as the China, the sarcenet, and the satin ribbons. Muffs and fur tippets are sold by the milliner, but the manufacture of them from the skin is a distinct business.

Velvet is used by milliners, and is now much in fashion. Velvet is a sort of stuff or silk, the nap of which is formed of part of the threads of the warp, which the workman puts on a channelled rule, and then cuts, by drawing a sharp steel tool along the channel of the ruler to the end of the warp.

*For the use of milliners and mantua makers who reside in the country, and also to gratify the curiosity of ladies in general, a work is published in London every month, entitled "The Monthly Fashion of London and Paris" containing from ten to fifteen fashionable dresses in each number, drawn from real life, in the first circles. Price 1s 6d each number.

THE FEATHER-WORKER

This is another business in which women are chiefly employed. Within these few years, the trade for feathers, especially for those worn by the military, has very greatly increased.

Before the feathers come into the hands of the person who makes them up for sale, they undergo several operations. They are curled, either by being baked, or by means of hot irons and when necessary, they are also dried.

The feathers principally in use are those of the ostrich, heron, the common cock, swan, peacock, and goose; of these, some are adapted to plumes with which hearses and horses are decorated at the funerals of the great; others are fitted for ornaments to the human head; to some we are indebted for the beds on which we lie, and to others for the pens with which we write.

Geese are plucked in some parts of Great Britain five times in a year; the first plucking is at Lady-day for feathers and quills, and four other pluckings are made between that time and Michaelmas for feathers only. In cold seasons many geese die by this barbarous custom. The fens in Lincolnshire abound with geese; and the produce of feathers is so great, that frequently three hundred bags, each containing one hundred weight and a half, are sent away in a year.

Military feathers are chiefly made of the *hackle* feathers, as they are called; these are plucked from the neck of the cock. The feathers of this bird are in great demand; his neck and back are clothed with long streaming feathers, intermixed with orange, black, and yellow; his tail is made up of stiff feathers, with two large ones waving over the rest in form of a sickle.

The plumage of the *wonderful Indian cock* is very beautiful, and consists of five different colours, viz. the black, white, green, red, and blue; and the tail is made up of twelve very beautiful feathers. But ostrich feathers are the most valuable; in their natural state they are mostly black and white; the largest feathers are at the extremities of their wings and tails.

The feathers of the ostrich require dyeing and dressing before they can be used as ornaments in ladies' head-dresses. The spoils of this bird are so valuable, that it is no wonder the human race, who reside in the vicinity of his resorts, have ever been his declared enemies, and constant pursuers. The Arabs are so sensible of the value of the ostrich, that they train their fleetest horses for the purpose of hunting them. When the ostrich perceives that he is pursued, he sets off at first in a gentle pace, as if insensible of his danger, or sure of escaping. In running, he keeps his wings, like arms, in constant motion, corresponding exactly with that of his legs. At length, when he is worn out with fatigue and hunger, he resolves to conceal himself; for which purpose he covers his head with the sand, or forces it into the first thicket he comes near, where he waits patiently until he is taken by his pursuers. The hunters always avoid killing their prey, because those feathers that are taken from the ostrich while he is alive are the most valuable; the others are dry, light, and liable to be spoiled by worms. Many tribes hunt and take them for the purpose of rendering them tame, that they may thereby obtain a supply of feathers, which is accomplished with very little trouble.

Round feathers are composed of a number of smaller ones; if they are taken from the cock's neck, they are neatly tied on wire with thread; but if they are small ostrich feathers, they are twisted round an upright wire. The single ostrich feathers have usually a small piece of wire at the end, for the purpose of fixing into the cap, turban, or hair. Women that work at this business can earn two shillings a day.

Feathers make a considerable article of commerce. Those imported from foreign countries, principally Poland and Germany, pay a heavy duty to the revenue. There is also a duty upon ostrich feathers, both in the undressed and also in the dressed state.

Feathers are divided into white, half white and grey. The best should be white, downy, void of large stems, fresh and sweet. Care should be taken that no sand be intermixed with them which is frequently done to weight.

THE GOLD-BEATER

Gold-leaf is gold beaten with a hammer, into exceedingly thin leaves. The fineness to which a body of gold may be reduced, is almost incredible. Mr. Boyle found that upwards of 50 square inches of gold, weighed but a single grain; and as a cubic inch of gold contains 4902 grains, the thickness of the gold-leaf was less than the two hundred and forty thousandth part of an inch.

Gold, to be made into leaf, is first melted in a crucible with some borax, it is then poured into an iron mould, from which it is taken and made red hot, and forged into a long plate, which is farther extended, by being passed repeatedly between polished rollers, till it becomes as thin as paper. It is now cut into pieces of equal size and weight, which are forged and well annealed to correct the stiffness which the metal has contracted in the hammering and flatting.

In farther extending these pieces into fine leaves, it is necessary to interpose some smooth body between them and the hammer, for softening the blow, and defending them from the rudeness of its immediate action; as also to place between every two of the pieces, some proper intermedium, which, while it prevents them from uniting together, or injuring one another, may suffer them freely to extend. For this gold-beaters use three kind of membranes; for the outside cover, common parchment made of sheep-skin; for interlaying with the gold, the closest vellum made of calf's skin; and afterwards, finer skins made of a thin substance stript off from the gut, slit open, and curiously prepared for the purpose: hence the name *gold-beater's skin*. The preparation of these membranes is a distinct business, practised only by a few persons in the kingdom.

Thus beating of the gold is performed on a smooth block of marble, weighing from two to six hundred weight; fitted into the middle of a wooden frame, so that the surface of the marble and the frame, may form one plane. Three of the sides are furnished with a high ledge; and the front, which is open, has a leathern flap fastened to it, which the gold beater takes before him as an apron for preserving the fragments of gold that fall off.

Three hammers are employed, all of them, with two round and somewhat convex faces, though the workmen seldom use more than one of the faces. The first hammer weighs fifteen or sixteen pounds, and is called the *cutch* hammer; the second is called the *shodering* hammer, and weighs twelve pounds, the third is the *finishing* hammer and weighs about ten pounds.

One hundred and fifty pieces of gold are interlaid with leaves of vellum, three or four inches square, one vellum leaf being placed between every two of the pieces, and about twenty more of the vellum leaves on the outsides; over these is drawn a parchment case, open at both ends; and over this, another in a contrary direction, so that the assemblage of gold and vellum leaves, is kept tight and close on all sides. The whole is beaten with the heaviest hammer, and every now and then turned upside down, till the gold is stretched to the extent of the vellum. The pieces, taken out from between the vellum leaves, are cut into four with a steel knife; and the six hundred divisions are next interlaid in the same manner, with pieces of ox-gut skins, five inches square. The beating is to be again repeated, till the golden plates have acquired the extent of the skins: when they are a second time to be divided into four. The instrument used for this division, is a piece of cane cut to an edge, the leaves being now so slight, that the moisture of the air, or the breadth condensing on a metallic knife, would occasion them to stick to it.

After a third beating in a similar way, the leaves are taken up by the end of a cane instrument, and being blown flat on a leathern cushion, and cut to a size, one by one with a square frame of cane, made of a proper sharpness; they are then fitted into books of twenty-five leaves each, the paper of which is well smoothed and rubbed with red-bole, to prevent their sticking to it.

The process of gold-beating is very much influenced by the weather; both damp and frost, are injurious to the operation.

Gold-leaf ought to be prepared from the finest gold, as the admixture of other metals, though in too small a proportion sensibly to affect the colour of the leaf, would dispose it to lose a part of its beauty in the air. Besides the greater hardness of alloyed gold, occasions as much, or even more, to be lost in point of time and labour, than can be gained by adulterating the metal.

Gold-leaf is applied, in the art of gilding, to the surface of bodies, and it is done in two ways. — Wood, leather, paper, and other like substances, are gilt by fastening on leaves of gold, by means of some cement; but metals are gilt by a chemical application of the gold to the surface. This last is called water-gilding.

CONTENTS of PART II